BETTER HOMES AND GARDENS®

COOKING FOR TODAY
CAKES

BETTER HOMES AND GARDENS® BOOKS
Des Moines

BETTER HOMES AND GARDENS® BOOKS
An Imprint of Meredith® Books

CAKES
Editor: Mary Major Williams
Writer: Joanne G. Fullan
Associate Art Director: Tom Wegner
Electronic Production Coordinator: Paula Forest
Test Kitchen Product Supervisors: Diana Nolin, Colleen Weeden
Food Stylists: Lynn Blanchard, Janet Pittman, Jennifer Peterson
Photographers: Mike Dieter, Scott Little
Production Manager: Douglas Johnston

Vice President and Editorial Director: Elizabeth P. Rice
Executive Editor: Kay Sanders
Art Director: Ernest Shelton
Managing Editor: Christopher Cavanaugh
Test Kitchen Director: Sharon Stilwell

President, Book Group: Joseph J. Ward
Vice President Retail Marketing: Jamie L. Martin
Vice President Direct Marketing: Timothy Jarrell

On the cover: Vanilla-Fudge Marble Cake (see recipe, page 141)

Meredith Corporation
Chairman of the Executive Committee: E. T. Meredith III
Chairman of the Board, President and Chief Executive Officer: Jack D. Rehm
President and Chief Operating Officer: William T. Kerr

WE CARE!

All of us at Better Homes and Gardens® Books are dedicated to providing you with the information and ideas you need to create tasty foods. We welcome your comments and suggestions. Write us at: Better Homes and Gardens® Books, Cookbook Editorial Department, RW-240, 1716 Locust St., Des Moines, IA 50309-3023

If you would like to order additional copies of any of our books,
call 1-800-678-2803 or check with your local bookstore.

Our seal assures you that every recipe in *Cakes* has been tested in the Better Homes and Gardens® Test Kitchen. This means that each recipe is practical and reliable, and meets our high standards of taste appeal. We guarantee your satisfaction with this book for as long as you own it.

Turning these pages is like touring your favorite bakery. You'll find a cake for any and every occasion, and even cakes for days with no occasion other than you want a treat. With 68 delightfully delicious recipes, you'll be hard put to decide just where to begin baking. We have velvet-crumbed chiffon cakes, light-as-a-feather angel food cakes, chocolate cakes in all shapes and sizes, and layer cakes in every flavor imaginable with an impressive assortment of fillings and frostings to match.

Some cakes are eminently suited to birthdays—a classic Ice Cream Cake with a choice of ice cream flavors or a Hot Milk Sponge Cake crowned with a fluffy pink frosting that's just right for a little girl's special day. Others, such as Banana Cake with Penuche Frosting, are iced right in the pan making them perfect choices to tote to a picnic or potluck supper. For breakfast or brunch, savor our Crumb-Crusted Lemon Coffee Cake or Cherry-Almond Coffee Cake. Enjoy old-fashioned favorites like Buttermilk Carrot Cake, Chocolate Fudge Cake, or a buttery rich Pound Cake. Or, sample something new, such as mint-frosted Grasshopper Cake or luscious Mocha Truffle Roll. The list goes on and on, but enough said. Start mixing!

CONTENTS

BEFORE YOU START

■ For all recipes in this book, use large eggs and regular margarine or butter. Do not use whipped butter, diet or low-calorie margarines, or the soft spreadable margarines or butter blends that are sold in tubs.

■ All ingredients, unless otherwise specified, should be at room temperature. Margarine, butter, shortening, cream cheese, eggs, milk, and other liquids should be measured first and then allowed to stand at room temperature for 30 minutes.

■ Separate eggs while they are still cold (the yolks are less likely to break), and then let them come to room temperature. If a yolk does break, be careful not to get any in the egg whites. Even a tiny speck of fat from a broken yolk will make it impossible to beat the whites to the stiff peaks necessary for angel food, sponge, and chiffon cakes.

■ Prepare the baking pans as directed in the recipe. For shortening-type cakes that are removed from their pans, the pans need to be greased and lightly floured. For those cakes that are left in their pans after baking, grease the pans without flouring them. Pans for angel food, sponge, and chiffon cakes should not be greased unless otherwise specified.

■ Preheat your oven before you begin to mix the ingredients. Most ovens require about 10 minutes to reach baking temperatures.

MEASURE FOR SUCCESS

Measuring Dry Ingredients: Use a dry measure with exactly the capacity you wish to measure. Spoon the ingredients lightly into the cup, then level off with the straight edge of a metal spatula. Do not pack dry ingredients except brown sugar which must be packed into the cup so it holds the shape of the measure when turned out.

Measuring Liquids: Use a standard glass or clear plastic measuring cup and place it on a level surface. Bend down so your eye is level with the marking you wish to read and fill the cup to the marking.

Measuring Shortening, Margarine, or Butter: Pack the shortening into a dry measuring cup with exactly the capacity you wish to measure. Run a spatula through the shortening in the measuring cup to remove any air pockets, then level off with the straight edge of a metal spatula or a knife. The easiest way to measure margarine or butter is to use a quarter-pound stick for ½ cup, half of the stick for ¼ cup, or one-eighth of a stick for 1 tablespoon.

SLICK TRICKS

Baking Three Layers with Only Two Pans: While baking the first two layers, keep the batter for the third covered and refrigerated. After you have removed the first two layers from the pans, wash the pans and prepare one to bake the remaining batter. Because the batter has been refrigerated, it may take a few extra minutes to bake.

Splitting Cake Layers: Insert eight toothpicks to mark the halfway point at equal intervals around the side of each layer to be split. Using the toothpicks as a cutting guide, slice each layer in half horizontally with a sharp, long-bladed knife.

Frosting Cakes: Use a pastry brush or your hand to brush loose crumbs from the cooled cake layers. Place one layer topside down on a cake plate. To keep the plate clean, slide strips of waxed paper just under the cake so the edge of the plate is covered. Using a metal spatula, spread about a fourth of the frosting over the layer. Place second layer, topside up, on frosted layer. Spread the sides of the cake with a thin coat of frosting to seal in the crumbs. Use about two-thirds of the remaining frosting to swirl a thicker layer over the sides. Spread and swirl remaining frosting on top of cake, joining frosted sides at edge of cake top. Carefully pull out waxed paper strips from under cake. When frosting a cake of three or more layers, always place the top layer topside up.

Freezing Cakes: Cool unfrosted cakes completely on wire racks before freezing them. Tightly wrap cooled cakes in foil or plastic wrap, then seal in plastic bags and freeze up to 4 months. To freeze a frosted cake, place the cake on a baking sheet and freeze until the frosting is firm before wrapping in foil or plastic wrap and sealing in a large plastic bag. *Do not* freeze a cake with a fluffy frosting or with a whipped cream filling or frosting. Store cakes in the freezer for 2 to 3 months.

Adjusting Recipes for High Altitude Baking: If you live more than 3,000 feet above sea level, use this chart to adjust cake ingredients. Try the smaller amount first, then make any necessary adjustments on your next cake.

Ingredient	3,000 feet	5,000 feet	7,000 feet
Liquid:			
Add for each cup	1 to 2 tablespoons	2 to 4 tablespoons	3 to 4 tablespoons
Baking powder:			
Decrease for each teaspoon	$\frac{1}{8}$ teaspoon	$\frac{1}{8}$ to $\frac{1}{4}$ teaspoon	$\frac{1}{4}$ teaspoon
Sugar:			
Decrease for each cup	0 to 1 tablespoon	0 to 2 tablespoons	1 to 3 tablespoons

For additional information, contact your county extension agent or write:
Colorado State University, Bulletin Room, Fort Collins, CO 80523.

PEAR-WALNUT COFFEE CAKE

A layer of chopped walnuts, cinnamon, and thin pear slices makes this velvety sour cream cake a breakfast or brunch delight.

1   medium pear or apple, peeled, cored, and sliced
1   teaspoon lemon juice
1¾   cups all-purpose flour
¾   teaspoon baking powder
½   teaspoon baking soda
¼   teaspoon salt
½   cup margarine or butter
1   cup granulated sugar
1   teaspoon vanilla
2   eggs
1   8-ounce carton dairy sour cream
    Walnut Filling and Topping

Grease a 9-inch springform pan or a 9x9x2-inch baking pan. Toss pear or apple slices with lemon juice. Stir together flour, baking powder, baking soda, and salt. Set aside.

In a large mixing bowl beat margarine or butter with an electric mixer on medium to high speed for 30 seconds or till softened. Add sugar and vanilla; beat till combined. Add eggs, one at a time, beating well after each. Alternately add flour mixture and sour cream, beating on low to medium speed after each addition just till combined. Pour *two-thirds* of the batter into prepared pan. Sprinkle with Walnut Filling. Arrange pear slices evenly over top. Spread remaining batter over pear slices. Sprinkle with Walnut Topping.

Bake in a 350° oven for 55 to 60 minutes or till a wooden toothpick inserted in center comes out clean. Cool in pan on wire rack 10 minutes. Remove sides from springform pan. Serve warm or cool completely on wire rack. Makes 12 servings.

Walnut Filling and Topping: In a mixing bowl stir together 1 cup chopped *walnuts*, ⅓ cup packed *brown sugar*, and 1 teaspoon ground *cinnamon*. Set aside ¾ *cup* of the mixture for Walnut Filling. For Walnut Topping, add ⅓ cup *all-purpose flour* and ¼ cup softened *margarine or butter* to the remaining mixture; stir till crumbly.

Nutrition facts per serving: 377 calories, 21 g total fat (5 g saturated fat), 43 mg cholesterol, 251 mg sodium, 43 g carbohydrate, 1 g fiber, 5 g protein.
Daily Value: 18% vitamin A, 2% vitamin C, 4% calcium, 10% iron.

ORANGE-RAISIN COFFEE CAKE

Orange yogurt imparts a zesty citrus flavor and extra moistness to this handsome cake.

2½ cups all-purpose flour
1 cup granulated sugar
1 tablespoon baking powder
½ teaspoon salt
¾ cup margarine or butter
2 teaspoons finely shredded orange peel
3 beaten eggs
1 8-ounce carton orange yogurt
⅓ cup milk
1 teaspoon vanilla
1 cup light raisins
  Orange Glaze

Grease and lightly flour a 10-inch fluted tube pan. Set aside.

In a large mixing bowl stir together flour, sugar, baking powder, and salt. Using a pastry blender or two knives, cut in margarine or butter till mixture resembles coarse crumbs. Stir in orange peel. Make a well in the center of the flour mixture.

In a small mixing bowl stir together eggs, yogurt, milk, and vanilla. Add yogurt mixture all at once to flour mixture. Stir just till moistened. Fold in raisins. Pour batter into prepared pan.

Bake in a 350° oven about 40 minutes or till a wooden toothpick inserted in the center comes out clean. Cool in pan on a wire rack for 10 minutes. Remove from pan. Cool completely on wire rack. Drizzle with Orange Glaze. Makes 12 to 16 servings.

Orange Glaze: In a small mixing bowl stir together 1 cup sifted *powdered sugar* and 3 to 4 teaspoons *orange juice or milk* to make glaze of a drizzling consistency.

Nutrition facts per serving: 371 calories, 13 g total fat (3 g saturated fat), 55 mg cholesterol, 346 mg sodium, 59 g carbohydrate, 1 g fiber, 6 g protein.
Daily Value: 17% vitamin A, 2% vitamin C, 12% calcium, 11% iron.

CHERRY-ALMOND COFFEE CAKE

Enjoy this buttery streusel-topped cake warm from the oven with a steaming cup of coffee or tea.

1⅓   cups all-purpose flour
1½   teaspoons baking powder
¼   teaspoon salt
¾   cup margarine or butter
¾   cup granulated sugar
½   teaspoon vanilla
½   teaspoon almond extract
3   eggs
1   16-ounce can pitted, dark sweet
      cherries, well drained
      Almond-Crumb Topping
2   tablespoons sliced almonds

Grease a 9x9x2-inch baking pan. Stir together flour, baking powder, and salt. Set aside.

In a large mixing bowl beat margarine or butter with an electric mixer on medium to high speed for 30 seconds or till softened. Add sugar, vanilla, and almond extract; beat till combined. Add eggs, one at a time, beating well after each. Gradually add flour mixture, beating on low to medium speed just till combined. Pour batter into prepared pan. Top with drained cherries. Sprinkle with Almond-Crumb Topping and almonds.

Bake in a 350° oven for 40 to 45 minutes or till a wooden toothpick inserted in center comes out clean. Serve warm or cool completely in pan on wire rack. Makes 9 servings.

Almond-Crumb Topping: Stir together ⅔ cup *all-purpose flour,* ¼ cup softened *margarine or butter,* 3 tablespoons *granulated sugar,* and ¼ teaspoon *almond extract* till crumbly.

Nutrition facts per serving: 428 calories, 23 g total fat (4 g saturated fat), 71 mg cholesterol, 323 mg sodium, 50 g carbohydrate, 1 g fiber, 6 g protein.
Daily Value: 28% vitamin A, 2% vitamin C, 2% calcium, 11% iron.

CRANBERRY-NUT COFFEE CAKE

A delectable sour cream cake, studded with tangy cranberries and coarsely chopped pecans, adds a festive touch to a brunch or coffee break.

2 cups all-purpose flour
1 teaspoon baking powder
1 teaspoon baking soda
¼ teaspoon salt
½ cup margarine or butter
1 cup packed brown sugar
1 teaspoon vanilla
2 eggs
1 8-ounce carton dairy sour cream
1 cup coarsely chopped cranberries
¾ cup coarsely chopped pecans
  Powdered Sugar Icing

Grease and lightly flour a 10-inch tube pan. Stir together flour, baking powder, baking soda, and salt. Set aside.

In a large mixing bowl beat margarine or butter with an electric mixer on medium to high speed about 30 seconds or till softened. Add brown sugar and vanilla; beat till combined. Add eggs, one at a time, beating well after each. Alternately add flour mixture and sour cream, beating on low to medium speed after each addition just till combined. Stir in cranberries and pecans. Pour into prepared pan.

Bake in a 350° oven for 50 to 55 minutes or till a wooden toothpick inserted in center comes out clean. Cool in pan on a wire rack for 6 minutes. Remove from pan. Cool completely on wire rack. Drizzle with Powdered Sugar Icing. Makes 12 servings.

Powdered Sugar Icing: In a small mixing bowl stir together 1 cup sifted *powdered sugar,* 1 tablespoon *milk,* and ¼ teaspoon *vanilla.* Stir in additional milk, if necessary, till icing is of drizzling consistency.

Nutrition facts per serving: 332 calories, 16 g total fat (4 g saturated fat), 43 mg cholesterol, 246 mg sodium, 44 g carbohydrate, 1 g fiber, 4 g protein.
Daily Value: 13% vitamin A, 2% vitamin C, 6% calcium, 10% iron.

CRUMB-CRUSTED LEMON COFFEE CAKE

The oh-so-good lemony spice cake bakes on top of a pecan shortbread crust!

2   cups all-purpose flour
1¼ cups granulated sugar
1½ teaspoons finely shredded lemon peel
½   teaspoon ground allspice or
        ¼ teaspoon ground cardamom
¼   teaspoon salt
⅔   cup margarine or butter
2   tablespoons finely chopped pecans
1   teaspoon baking powder
¼   teaspoon baking soda
1   beaten egg
½   cup lemon or vanilla lowfat yogurt
1   tablespoon lemon juice
½   cup finely chopped pecans

Grease a 9x9x2-inch baking pan. Set aside.

In a large mixing bowl stir together flour, sugar, lemon peel, allspice or cardamom, and salt. Using a pastry blender, cut in margarine or butter till mixture resembles coarse crumbs. For crust, remove *1 cup* of the crumb mixture; stir in 2 tablespoons finely chopped pecans. Pat the nut mixture into the bottom of prepared pan. Bake in a 350° oven for 8 minutes.

Meanwhile, stir baking powder and baking soda into the remaining crumb mixture. Make a well in the center. Stir together beaten egg, yogurt, and lemon juice. Add egg mixture all at once to the crumb mixture. Stir just till moistened (batter should be lumpy). Spoon batter over crust. Sprinkle with the ½ cup finely chopped pecans.

Bake in a 350° oven for 35 to 40 minutes or till a wooden toothpick inserted in center comes out clean. Cool in pan on a wire rack for 15 minutes. Cut into squares and serve warm. Makes 9 servings.

Nutrition facts per serving: 393 calories, 20 g total fat (3 g saturated fat), 24 mg cholesterol, 307 mg sodium, 51 g carbohydrate, 1 g fiber, 5 g protein.
Daily Value: 18% vitamin A, 2% vitamin C, 6% calcium, 10% iron.

APPLE CAKE

Generously rippled with apple slices and cinnamon and drizzled with powdered sugar icing, this luscious cake is especially welcome for breakfast or brunch on crisp autumn mornings.

¼ **cup granulated sugar**
2 **tablespoons all-purpose flour**
1½ **teaspoons ground cinnamon**
5 **cups sliced, peeled cooking apples**
2½ **cups all-purpose flour**
1½ **cups granulated sugar**
1½ **teaspoons baking powder**
½ **teaspoon baking soda**
1 **cup cooking oil**
4 **eggs**
¼ **cup orange juice**
2 **teaspoons vanilla**
  Powdered Sugar Icing (see recipe, page 13)

Grease and lightly flour a 10-inch fluted tube pan. In a large mixing bowl combine ¼ cup sugar, 2 tablespoons flour, and cinnamon. Add apples; toss to coat. Set aside.

In a large mixing bowl combine 2½ cups flour, 1½ cups sugar, baking powder, and baking soda. Add oil, eggs, orange juice, and vanilla; beat with an electric mixer on low to medium speed about 30 seconds. Beat on medium speed 2 minutes. Pour *one-third* of the batter (about 1½ cups) into the prepared pan. Top with *half* of the apple mixture. Spoon another *one-third* of the batter over apples in pan; top with remaining apples. Spoon remaining batter over apples.

Bake in a 350° oven about 1¼ hours or till a wooden toothpick inserted in center comes out clean. Cool in pan on wire rack for 15 minutes. Remove from pan. Cool completely on a wire rack. Drizzle with Powdered Sugar Icing. Let cake stand for 1 to 2 hours before slicing. Makes 16 servings.

Nutrition facts per serving: 338 calories, 15 g total fat (2 g saturated fat), 53 mg cholesterol, 56 mg sodium, 48 g carbohydrate, 1 g fiber, 4 g protein.
Daily Value: 2% vitamin A, 3% vitamin C, 1% calcium, 8% iron.

BANANA CAKE WITH PENUCHE FROSTING

For a combination that's hard to beat, frost this easy-to-make cake right in the pan with a creamy brown sugar frosting.

2½   cups all-purpose flour
1½   cups granulated sugar
1½   teaspoons baking powder
1   teaspoon baking soda
½   teaspoon salt
1   cup mashed ripe bananas (about 3)
⅔   cup buttermilk or sour milk*
½   cup shortening
1   teaspoon vanilla
2   eggs
     Penuche Frosting
     Chopped nuts (optional)

Grease a 13x9x2-inch baking pan. Set aside.

In a large mixing bowl combine flour, sugar, baking powder, baking soda, and salt. Add bananas, buttermilk or sour milk, shortening, and vanilla. Beat with an electric mixer on low speed till combined. Add eggs; beat 2 minutes on medium speed. Pour into prepared pan.

Bake in a 350° oven about 35 minutes or till a wooden toothpick inserted in center comes out clean. Cool completely in pan on a wire rack. Frost with Penuche Frosting. Immediately sprinkle with chopped nuts, if desired. Makes 12 to 16 servings.

Penuche Frosting: In a medium saucepan melt ⅓ cup *butter or margarine* over medium heat. Stir in ⅔ cup packed *brown sugar.* Cook and stir till bubbly. Remove from heat. Add 3 tablespoons *milk,* beating vigorously till smooth. By hand, beat in enough sifted powdered sugar (about 2½ cups) to make frosting of spreading consistency. Frost cake immediately.

Note: For sour milk, place 2 teaspoons lemon juice or vinegar in a measuring cup. Add enough whole milk to make ⅔ cup.

Nutrition facts per serving: 470 calories, 15 g total fat (6 g saturated fat), 50 mg cholesterol, 274 mg sodium, 82 g carbohydrate, 1 g fiber, 4 g protein.
Daily Value: 6% vitamin A, 3% vitamin C, 3% calcium, 10% iron.

UPSIDE-DOWN PINEAPPLE-ORANGE CAKE

For a twist on pineapple upside-down cake, we added mandarin orange sections, using half a can of pineapple slices and half a can of orange sections. If you prefer to make the cake with just one fruit, use a whole can.

6   tablespoons margarine or butter
⅔   cup packed brown sugar
1½ teaspoons finely shredded orange peel
1   11-ounce can mandarin orange
        segments, drained
1   8-ounce can pineapple slices, drained
        and cut in half crosswise
1⅓ cups all-purpose flour
1¼ teaspoons baking powder
½   teaspoon salt
6   tablespoons margarine or butter
1   cup granulated sugar
¼   teaspoon almond extract
2   eggs
⅔   cup dairy sour cream
    Sweetened Whipped Cream
        (see recipe, page 22)

In a medium saucepan combine 6 tablespoons margarine or butter, brown sugar, and orange peel. Cook and stir over medium heat till mixture is bubbly. Pour into an ungreased 9x9x2-inch baking pan.

Drain the mandarin orange segments and pineapple. Cut *half* of the pineapple slices in half. Arrange the half slices of pineapple and *half* of the orange segments in pan. (Reserve remaining orange segments and pineapple slices for another use.) Combine flour, baking powder, and salt. Set aside.

In a large mixing bowl beat 6 tablespoons margarine or butter with an electric mixer on medium to high speed about 30 seconds or till softened. Add granulated sugar and almond extract; beat till combined. Add eggs, one at a time, beating well after each. Alternately add flour mixture and sour cream, beating on low to medium speed after each addition just till combined. Spoon the batter evenly over the fruit in the pan.

Bake in a 350° oven for 35 to 40 minutes or till a wooden toothpick inserted in center comes out clean. Cool in the pan on a wire rack for 5 minutes. Invert onto serving plate. Serve warm. Top with Sweetened Whipped Cream, if desired. Makes 8 servings.

Nutrition facts per serving: 455 calories, 21 g total fat (5 g saturated fat), 61 mg cholesterol, 371 mg sodium, 64 g carbohydrate, 1 g fiber, 4 g protein.
Daily Value: 26% vitamin A, 1% vitamin C, 4% calcium, 9% iron.

OLD-FASHIONED GINGERBREAD

Freshly grated gingerroot gives extra zing to this lovely, fine-textured gingerbread. Try a piece warm and topped with a dollop of whipped cream.

1½   cups all-purpose flour
½   teaspoon baking powder
½   teaspoon baking soda
½   teaspoon ground cinnamon
½   teaspoon salt
⅛   teaspoon ground cloves
½   cup shortening
¼   cup packed brown sugar
1   egg
½   cup molasses
2   teaspoons grated fresh gingerroot or
    ¾ teaspoon ground ginger
½   cup boiling water
    Sweetened Whipped Cream (optional)

Grease an 8x8x2-inch baking pan. Combine flour, baking powder, baking soda, cinnamon, salt, and cloves. Set aside.

In a large mixing bowl beat shortening with an electric mixer on medium to high speed about 30 seconds or till softened. Add brown sugar; beat till combined. Add egg, molasses, and gingerroot or ground ginger; beat 1 minute. Alternately add flour mixture and boiling water, beating on low to medium speed after each addition just till combined. Pour batter into prepared pan.

Bake in a 350° oven 30 to 35 minutes or till a wooden toothpick inserted in center comes out clean. Cool slightly in pan on wire rack. Serve warm and, if desired, top with Sweetened Whipped Cream. Makes 9 servings.

Sweetened Whipped Cream: In a chilled medium mixing bowl combine 1 cup *whipping cream,* 2 tablespoons *granulated sugar,* and ½ teaspoon *vanilla.* Beat with an electric mixer on medium to high speed till soft peaks form.

Nutrition facts per serving: 247 calories, 12 g total fat (3 g saturated fat), 24 mg cholesterol, 198 mg sodium, 32 g carbohydrate, 1 g fiber, 3 g protein.
Daily Value: 1% vitamin A, 0% vitamin C, 3% calcium, 12% iron.

BUSY-DAY CAKE

No time to bake? Stir up this one-bowl cake in only minutes with easy-to-keep-on-hand ingredients. Another time, skip the topping and serve it with fresh fruit and whipped cream.

1⅓   cups all-purpose flour
⅔   cup granulated sugar
2   teaspoons baking powder
⅔   cup milk
¼   cup margarine or butter, softened
1   egg
1   teaspoon vanilla
   Broiled Coconut Topping

Grease and flour an 8x1½-inch round baking pan. Set aside.

In a large mixing bowl combine flour, sugar, and baking powder. Add milk, margarine or butter, egg, and vanilla. Beat with an electric mixer on low speed for 30 seconds. Beat on medium speed for 1 minute. Pour batter into prepared pan.

Bake in a 350° oven for 25 to 30 minutes or till a wooden toothpick inserted in center comes out clean. Spread Broiled Coconut Topping over warm cake. Broil about 4 inches from heat for 3 to 4 minutes or till topping is golden. Cool slightly in pan on a wire rack. Serve warm. Makes 8 servings.

Broiled Coconut Topping: In a medium bowl stir together ¼ cup packed *brown sugar* and 2 tablespoons softened *margarine or butter*. Stir in 1 tablespoon *milk*. Then, stir in ½ cup *flaked coconut*, and, if desired, ¼ cup *chopped nuts*.

Nutrition facts per serving: 281 calories, 11 g total fat (3 g saturated fat), 28 mg cholesterol, 128 mg sodium, 42 g carbohydrate, 1 g fiber, 4 g protein.
Daily Value: 13% vitamin A, 0% vitamin C, 4% calcium, 8% iron.

OATMEAL CAKE

The natural goodness of rolled oats together with brown sugar and cinnamon give this old-fashioned cake its wonderful flavor.

1¼ cups boiling water
1 cup rolled oats
2 cups all-purpose flour
2 teaspoons baking powder
¾ teaspoon ground cinnamon
½ teaspoon baking soda
½ teaspoon salt
¼ teaspoon ground nutmeg
½ cup margarine or butter, softened
¾ cup granulated sugar
½ cup packed brown sugar
1 teaspoon vanilla
2 eggs
Broiled Nut Topping

Grease and lightly flour a 9-inch springform pan. Pour boiling water over oats. Stir till combined; let stand 20 minutes. Combine flour, baking powder, cinnamon, baking soda, salt, and nutmeg. Set aside.

In a large mixing bowl beat margarine or butter with an electric mixer on medium to high speed for 30 seconds or till softened. Add granulated sugar, brown sugar, and vanilla; beat till combined. Add eggs, one at a time, beating well after each. Alternately add flour mixture and oatmeal mixture, beating on low to medium speed after each addition just till combined. Pour batter into prepared pan.

Bake in a 350° oven for 40 to 45 minutes or till a wooden toothpick inserted in center comes out clean. Cool in pan on a wire rack for 20 minutes. Remove sides of pan; cool on wire rack for at least 1 hour more. Transfer cake to a baking sheet. Spread Broiled Nut Topping over warm cake. Broil about 4 inches from heat for 2 to 3 minutes or till topping is bubbly and golden. Cool on a wire rack before serving. Makes 12 servings.

Broiled Nut Topping: In a medium saucepan combine ¼ cup *margarine or butter* and 2 tablespoons *half-and-half, light cream, or milk.* Cook and stir till margarine or butter melts. Add ½ cup packed *brown sugar;* stir till sugar dissolves. Remove from heat. Stir in ¾ cup chopped *pecans or walnuts* and ⅓ cup *flaked coconut.*

Nutrition facts per serving: 388 calories, 18 g total fat (4 g saturated fat), 36 mg cholesterol, 296 mg sodium, 52 g carbohydrate, 1 g fiber, 5 g protein.
Daily Value: 16% vitamin A, 0% vitamin C, 3% calcium, 12% iron.

SPONGE CAKE WITH BROILED MACADAMIA-COCONUT TOPPING

Hot milk sponge cake crowned with an extra-easy broiled topping—so delicious everyone will want seconds!

1   cup all-purpose flour
1   teaspoon baking powder
2   eggs
½   teaspoon vanilla
1   cup granulated sugar
½   cup milk
2   tablespoons margarine or butter
    Broiled Macadamia-Coconut Topping

Grease a 9x9x2-inch baking pan. Combine flour and baking powder. Set aside.

In a large mixing bowl beat eggs and vanilla with an electric mixer on high speed about 4 minutes or till thick and lemon-colored. Gradually add sugar, beating on medium speed about 5 minutes or till sugar is almost dissolved. Gradually add the flour mixture, beating on low to medium speed just till combined. In a small saucepan heat milk and margarine or butter till the margarine melts. Add milk mixture to egg mixture, stirring just till combined. Pour batter into prepared pan.

Bake in a 350° oven for 25 to 30 minutes or till top springs back when lightly touched. Cool in pan on wire rack for 10 minutes. Carefully spread Broiled Macadamia-Coconut Frosting over warm cake. Broil about 4 inches from the heat for 2 to 3 minutes or till lightly browned and bubbly. Cool completely in pan on wire rack. Makes 9 servings.

Broiled Macadamia-Coconut Topping: In a small mixing bowl stir together ½ cup *flaked coconut*, ¼ cup packed *brown sugar*, ¼ cup chopped *macadamia nuts or slivered almonds*, 2 tablespoons *margarine or butter*, and 1 tablespoon *milk*.

Nutrition facts per serving: 271 calories, 11 g total fat (3 g saturated fat), 48 mg cholesterol, 87 mg sodium, 41 g carbohydrate, 1 g fiber, 4 g protein.
Daily Value: 9% vitamin A, 0% vitamin C, 3% calcium, 6% iron.

NUTMEG CAKE WITH LEMON SAUCE

Another time, savor this light spice cake with Penuche Frosting (see recipe, page 18)—perfect for lunch-box treats or after-school snacks.

2   cups all-purpose flour
1   teaspoon ground nutmeg
1   teaspoon baking powder
1   teaspoon baking soda
¼   teaspoon salt
¼   cup margarine or butter
¼   cup shortening
1½ cups granulated sugar
½   teaspoon vanilla
3   eggs
1   cup buttermilk or sour milk*
    Lemon Sauce

Grease a 13x9x2-inch baking pan. Combine flour, nutmeg, baking powder, baking soda, and salt. Set aside.

In a large mixing bowl beat together margarine or butter and shortening with an electric mixer on medium to high speed about 30 seconds or till softened. Add sugar and vanilla; beat till combined. Add eggs, one at a time, beating well after each. Alternately add flour mixture and buttermilk or sour milk, beating on low speed after each addition just till combined. Pour batter into prepared pan.

Bake in a 350° oven for 30 to 35 minutes or till a wooden toothpick inserted in center comes out clean. Cool slightly in pan on wire rack. Serve warm with warm Lemon Sauce. Makes 12 servings.

Lemon Sauce: In a small saucepan stir together ¾ cup *granulated sugar,* 5 teaspoons *cornstarch,* and dash *salt.* Stir in 1 cup *water.* Cook and stir over medium heat till thickened and bubbly; cook and stir 2 minutes more. Remove from heat. Stir in 2 tablespoons *margarine or butter,* 1 teaspoon finely shredded *lemon peel,* 3 tablespoons *lemon juice,* and, if desired, 1 drop *yellow food coloring.*

Note: For sour milk, place 1 tablespoon lemon juice or vinegar in a measuring cup. Add enough whole milk to make 1 cup.

Nutrition facts per serving: 338 calories, 12 g total fat (3 g saturated fat), 54 mg cholesterol, 297 mg sodium, 55 g carbohydrate, 1 g fiber, 4 g protein.
Daily Value: 9% vitamin A, 3% vitamin C, 5% calcium, 7% iron.

APPLESAUCE CAKE WITH BROWNED BUTTER FROSTING

Raisins, nuts, and a blend of spices make this dessert a perennial favorite. After icing the cake, pull the tines of a fork through the top of the frosting to create a lattice pattern as shown in the photograph.

2½ cups all-purpose flour
1½ teaspoons baking powder
1 teaspoon ground cinnamon
¾ teaspoon ground nutmeg
½ teaspoon salt
½ teaspoon ground cloves
¼ teaspoon baking soda
½ cup margarine or butter
2 cups granulated sugar
2 eggs
1½ cups applesauce
½ cup raisins
½ cup chopped walnuts
Browned Butter Frosting

Grease a 13x9x2-inch baking pan. Combine flour, baking powder, cinnamon, nutmeg, salt, cloves, and baking soda. Set aside.

In a large mixing bowl beat margarine or butter with an electric mixer on medium to high speed about 30 seconds or till softened. Add sugar; beat till combined. Add eggs, one at a time, beating well after each. Alternately add flour mixture and applesauce, beating on low to medium speed after each addition just till combined. Stir in raisins and walnuts. Pour batter into prepared pan.

Bake in a 350° oven for 35 to 40 minutes or till a wooden toothpick inserted in center comes out clean. Cool completely in pan on a wire rack. Frost with Browned Butter Frosting. Makes 12 servings.

Browned Butter Frosting: In a small saucepan heat ½ cup *margarine or butter* over low heat till melted; continue heating till margarine or butter turns a delicate brown. Remove from heat; pour into small mixing bowl. Add 4 cups sifted *powdered sugar*, 2 tablespoons *milk*, and 1 teaspoon *vanilla*; beat with an electric mixer on low speed till combined. Beat on medium to high speed, adding additional milk, if necessary, to make frosting of a spreading consistency.

Nutrition facts per serving: 572 calories, 20 g total fat (4 g saturated fat), 36 mg cholesterol, 354 mg sodium, 98 g carbohydrate, 1 g fiber, 5 g protein. Daily Value: 20% vitamin A, 1% vitamin C, 5% calcium, 11% iron.

COCONUT-ALMOND PRALINE CAKE

The frosting for this three-tiered beauty is a cooked one that must be cooled until it's thick enough to spread. To speed the cooling process, set the pan of frosting in a bowl of ice water.

3 cups all-purpose flour
2 teaspoons baking powder
½ teaspoon salt
¼ teaspoon baking soda
½ cup margarine or butter
1 cup granulated sugar
1 cup packed brown sugar
1½ teaspoons vanilla
¼ teaspoon almond extract
2 eggs
1½ cups milk
½ cup flaked coconut, toasted
   Coconut-Almond Praline Frosting

Grease and lightly flour three 9x1½-inch round baking pans. Combine flour, baking powder, salt, and baking soda. Set aside.

In a large mixing bowl beat margarine or butter with an electric mixer on medium to high speed about 30 seconds or till softened. Add granulated sugar, brown sugar, vanilla, and almond extract; beat till combined. Add eggs, one at a time, beating well after each. Alternately add flour mixture and milk, beating on low speed after each addition just till combined. Stir in toasted coconut. Pour batter into prepared pans.

Bake in a 350° oven about 25 minutes or till a wooden toothpick inserted in centers comes out clean. Cool in pans on wire racks for 10 minutes. Remove from pans. Cool completely on wire racks. Spread Coconut-Almond Praline Frosting over the top of each layer; stack layers. Store, covered, in refrigerator. Makes 12 servings.

Coconut-Almond Praline Frosting: In a medium saucepan stir together 1 *egg,* 1 *egg yolk,* and 1 cup *granulated sugar* till well combined. Add 1 cup *evaporated milk,* 6 tablespoons *margarine or butter,* and ¼ teaspoon *almond extract.* Cook and stir over medium heat about 8 minutes or till thickened and bubbly. Stir in 1 cup toasted slivered *almonds,* chopped, and ¾ cup *flaked coconut.* Cool till frosting is thick enough to spread.

Nutrition facts per serving: 583 calories, 25 g total fat (6 g saturated fat), 79 mg cholesterol, 403 mg sodium, 83 g carbohydrate, 2 g fiber, 10 g protein.
Daily Value: 24% vitamin A, 1% vitamin C, 17% calcium, 17% iron.

SWEDISH SPICE CAKE

A fluffy maple frosting is the perfect accent for this brown sugar and spice cake.

2 cups all-purpose flour
1 teaspoon baking soda
1 teaspoon ground cinnamon
¼ teaspoon ground ginger
¼ teaspoon ground nutmeg
¼ teaspoon ground cloves
½ cup margarine or butter
1½ cups packed brown sugar
2 eggs
1 8-ounce carton dairy sour cream
Fluffy Maple Frosting

Grease and lightly flour two 8x1½-inch or 9x1½-inch round baking pans. Combine flour, baking soda, cinnamon, ginger, nutmeg, and cloves. Set aside.

In a large mixing bowl beat margarine or butter with an electric mixer on medium to high speed about 30 seconds or till softened. Add brown sugar; beat till combined. Add eggs, one at a time, beating well after each. Alternately add flour mixture and sour cream, beating on low to medium speed after each addition just till combined. Pour batter into prepared pans.

Bake in a 350° oven for 25 to 30 minutes or till a wooden toothpick inserted in centers comes out clean. Cool in pans on wire racks for 10 minutes. Remove from pans. Cool completely on wire racks. Fill and frost cake with Fluffy Maple Frosting. Makes 12 servings.

Fluffy Maple Frosting: In a medium saucepan combine 1 cup *granulated sugar*, ⅓ cup *water*, and ¼ teaspoon *cream of tartar*. Cook and stir over medium heat till bubbly and sugar dissolves. Remove from heat. In a small mixing bowl beat 2 *egg whites*, 1 teaspoon *vanilla*, and ½ teaspoon *maple flavoring* with an electric mixer on high speed till soft peaks form (tips curl). Slowly pour hot syrup over egg white mixture while beating constantly on high speed about 7 minutes or till stiff glossy peaks form (tips stand straight). Frost immediately.

Nutrition facts per serving: 364 calories, 13 g total fat (4 g saturated fat), 44 mg cholesterol, 236 mg sodium, 60 g carbohydrate, 1 g fiber, 4 g protein.
Daily Value: 15% vitamin A, 0% vitamin C, 4% calcium, 10% iron.

ORANGE CAKE

A velvety chocolate frosting sets off the sunny citrus flavor of this yellow butter cake. Enjoy a slice topped with a scoop of orange sherbet.

2¾ **cups all-purpose flour**
2   **teaspoons baking powder**
½   **teaspoon salt**
¼   **teaspoon baking soda**
½   **cup margarine or butter**
1¾ **cups granulated sugar**
1   **teaspoon vanilla**
2   **eggs**
1   **cup milk**
2   **tablespoons finely shredded orange peel (set aside)**
¼   **cup orange juice**
    Chocolate Velvet Frosting
    Orange peel shreds (optional)

Grease and flour two 9x1½-inch or two 8x1½-inch round baking pans. Combine flour, baking powder, salt, and baking soda. Set aside.

In a large bowl beat margarine with an electric mixer on medium to high speed till softened. Beat in sugar and vanilla till combined. Add eggs, one at a time, beating well after each. Combine milk and orange juice. Alternately add flour mixture and milk mixture, beating on low to medium speed after each addition just till combined. Stir in finely shredded orange peel. Pour into prepared pans.

Bake in a 350° oven for 30 to 35 minutes or till a wooden toothpick inserted in centers comes out clean. Cool in pans on wire racks for 10 minutes. Remove from pans. Cool completely on wire racks.

Fill and frost cake with Chocolate Velvet Frosting. If desired, pipe decorative borders around top and bottom of cake and sprinkle cake with orange peel shreds. Store, covered, in refrigerator. Serves 12.

Chocolate Velvet Frosting: Beat together ¼ cup *water* and 3 *egg yolks*. In top of a double boiler placed over boiling water (upper pan should not touch the water) melt one 12-ounce package (2 cups) *semisweet chocolate pieces.* Using a wire whisk, stir yolk mixture all at once into chocolate. Cook and stir about 5 minutes or till smooth and slightly thickened. Remove from heat; cool to room temperature. In a large bowl beat 1 cup *margarine or butter* with an electric mixer on medium to high speed till softened. Gradually beat in 1¼ cups sifted *powdered sugar* and 1½ teaspoons *vanilla* till well mixed. Beat in cooled chocolate mixture. Beat till smooth and creamy. If frosting is too soft, chill just till stiff enough to spread; beat before using.

Nutrition facts per serving: 629 calories, 34 g total fat (5 g saturated fat), 90 mg cholesterol, 468 mg sodium, 81 g carbohydrate, 1 g fiber, 7 g protein.
Daily Value: 39% vitamin A, 6% vitamin C, 9% calcium, 15% iron.

ITALIAN CREME CAKE

Stacked three layers high, this deliciously moist cake is studded with coconut and pecans and swirled with an extra-rich cream cheese frosting.

1¾ cups all-purpose flour
1½ teaspoons baking powder
¼ teaspoon baking soda
½ cup margarine or butter
⅓ cup shortening
1¾ cups granulated sugar
1 teaspoon vanilla
4 egg yolks
¾ cup buttermilk or sour milk*
1 3½-ounce can flaked coconut
    (1⅓ cups), chopped
1 cup finely chopped pecans
4 egg whites
    Cream Cheese Frosting

Grease and lightly flour three 8x1½-inch round baking pans. Combine flour, baking powder, and baking soda. Set aside.

In a large mixing bowl beat margarine or butter and shortening with an electric mixer on medium to high speed about 30 seconds or till softened. Add sugar and vanilla; beat till combined. Add egg yolks; beat well. Alternately add flour mixture and buttermilk or sour milk, beating on low to medium speed after each addition just till combined. Stir in coconut and pecans. Thoroughly wash beaters.

In a small mixing bowl beat egg whites on high speed till stiff peaks form (tips stand straight). Stir about *one-third* of the egg whites into batter to lighten. Gently fold remaining egg whites into batter. Pour batter into prepared pans.

Bake in a 350° oven for 25 to 30 minutes or till a toothpick inserted in centers comes out clean. Cool on wire racks 10 minutes. Remove from pans. Cool completely on wire racks. Fill and frost cake with Cream Cheese Frosting. Store, covered, in the refrigerator. Serves 12.

Cream Cheese Frosting: Beat 12 ounces *cream cheese,* 6 tablespoons *margarine or butter,* and 1½ teaspoons *vanilla* with an electric mixer on medium to high speed till fluffy. Gradually add 3 cups sifted *powdered sugar;* beat well. Gradually beat in additional sifted powdered sugar (2¾ to 3 cups) to make frosting of a spreading consistency.

Note: For sour milk, place 2 teaspoons lemon juice or vinegar in a measuring cup. Add enough whole milk to make ¾ cup.

Nutrition facts per serving: 759 calories, 40 g total fat (14 g saturated fat), 103 mg cholesterol, 352 mg sodium, 97 g carbohydrate, 2 g fiber, 8 g protein.
Daily Value: 39% vitamin A, 0% vitamin C, 8% calcium, 12% iron.

ALL-AMERICAN LAYER CAKE

This all-American favorite makes a fitting dessert for the Fourth of July.

2¾ cups all-purpose flour
2½ teaspoons baking powder
¼ teaspoon salt
½ cup margarine or butter
1¾ cups granulated sugar
1½ teaspoons vanilla
2 eggs
1¼ cups milk
Chocolate Butter Frosting or Vanilla
Butter Frosting

Grease and lightly flour three 8x1½-inch or two 9x1½-inch round baking pans. Combine flour, baking powder, and salt. Set aside.

In a large mixing bowl beat margarine or butter with an electric mixer on medium to high speed about 30 seconds or till softened. Add sugar and vanilla; beat till combined. Add eggs, one at a time, beating well after each. Alternately add flour mixture and milk, beating on low to medium speed after each addition just till combined. Pour batter into prepared pans.

Bake in a 350° oven 20 to 25 minutes for 8-inch pans or 25 to 30 minutes for 9-inch pans or till a wooden toothpick inserted in centers comes out clean. Cool in pans on wire racks for 10 minutes. Remove from pans. Cool completely on wire racks. Fill and frost with Chocolate Butter Frosting or Vanilla Butter Frosting. Serves 12 to 16.

Chocolate Butter Frosting: In a medium saucepan heat and stir 4 ounces cut up *unsweetened chocolate* and ¼ cup *margarine or butter* over low heat till melted. Remove from heat; cool 10 minutes. Gradually add 3 cups sifted *powdered sugar,* ¼ cup *milk,* and ¼ teaspoon *vanilla,* beating till smooth. Add additional milk, if necessary, to make frosting of spreading consistency.

Vanilla Butter Frosting: In a small mixing bowl beat 6 tablespoons *margarine or butter* till fluffy. Beat in one 1-pound box (about 4½ cups) *powdered sugar,* sifted; ¼ cup *milk;* and 1½ teaspoons *vanilla* till well combined. Add additional milk, if necessary, to make frosting of spreading consistency.

Nutrition facts per serving: 484 calories, 18 g total fat (5 g saturated fat), 38 mg cholesterol, 281 mg sodium, 79 g carbohydrate, 1 g fiber, 6 g protein.
Daily Value: 17% vitamin A, 0% vitamin C, 10% calcium, 14% iron.

ALMOND CLOUD TORTE

This almond-scented cake is named for the fluffy cloudlike frosting—a heavenly blend of whipped cream, cream cheese, and even more almond flavor.

2	cups all-purpose flour
1¼	teaspoons baking powder
½	teaspoon salt
⅔	cup margarine or butter
1⅔	cups granulated sugar
1	teaspoon vanilla
¼	teaspoon almond extract
4	eggs
⅔	cup milk
3	tablespoons almond liqueur or cream sherry
⅔	cup slivered almonds, toasted Almond Cream

Grease and lightly flour three 9x1½-inch or 8x1½-inch round baking pans. Combine flour, baking powder, and salt. Set aside.

In a large mixing bowl beat margarine or butter with an electric mixer on medium to high speed about 30 seconds or till softened. Gradually add sugar, vanilla, and almond extract; beat till combined. Add eggs, one at a time, beating well after each. Alternately add flour mixture and milk, beating on low to medium speed after each addition just till combined. Pour batter into prepared pans.

Bake in a 350° oven for 20 to 25 minutes or till a wooden toothpick inserted in centers comes out clean. Cool in pans on wire racks for 10 minutes. Remove from pans. Cool completely on wire racks. Brush the layers with almond liqueur or cream sherry.

Chop *half* of the almonds. Stir chopped almonds into *1 cup* of the Almond Cream; spread over the tops of two of the cake layers. Stack the layers. Top with remaining layer. Frost sides and top of cake with remaining Almond Cream. Sprinkle with remaining almonds. Store, covered, in refrigerator. Makes 12 servings.

Almond Cream: In a small mixing bowl beat two 3-ounce packages *cream cheese* with an electric mixer on medium to high speed about 30 seconds or till softened. Add ⅓ cup *granulated sugar*, ½ teaspoon *vanilla*, and ¼ teaspoon *almond extract;* beat till smooth. Gradually add 1½ cups *whipping cream*. Continue beating till soft peaks form and frosting is thick enough to spread.

Nutrition facts per serving: 528 calories, 32 g total fat (13 g saturated fat), 128 mg cholesterol, 329 mg sodium, 54 g carbohydrate, 1 g fiber, 8 g protein.
Daily Value: 35% vitamin A, 0% vitamin C, 9% calcium, 10% iron.

BUTTERMILK CARROT CAKE

Time to indulge! This deluxe version of carrot cake is topped with not one, but two different icings—a buttermilk glaze and a cream cheese-walnut frosting.

2	cups all-purpose flour
2	cups granulated sugar
2	teaspoons baking soda
1½	teaspoons ground cinnamon
1	teaspoon baking powder
¼	teaspoon salt
4	medium carrots, shredded (2 cups)
1	8¼-ounce can crushed pineapple, drained
1	cup chopped walnuts
3	eggs
½	cup coconut
¼	cup buttermilk or sour milk*
¼	cup cooking oil
1	teaspoon vanilla
	Buttermilk Glaze
	Nutty Cream Cheese Frosting
16	walnut halves (optional)

Grease and lightly flour two 9x1½-inch round baking pans. Set aside.

In a large mixing bowl combine flour, sugar, baking soda, cinnamon, baking powder, and salt. Add shredded carrots, pineapple, chopped walnuts, eggs, coconut, buttermilk or sour milk, cooking oil, and vanilla. Stir till combined. Pour batter in prepared pans.

Bake in a 350° oven for 40 to 45 minutes or till tops spring back when touched lightly. Immediately pour Buttermilk Glaze evenly over cakes in pans. Cool in pans on wire racks for 15 minutes. Remove from pans; cool completely on wire racks. Fill and frost with Nutty Cream Cheese Frosting. Top with walnut halves, if desired. Store in the refrigerator. Makes 16 servings.

Buttermilk Glaze: In a medium saucepan combine ½ cup *granulated sugar,* ¼ cup *buttermilk or sour milk*,* ¼ cup *margarine or butter,* and 2 teaspoons *light corn syrup.* Bring to boiling; reduce heat. Cook and stir for 4 minutes. Remove from heat; stir in ½ teaspoon *vanilla.*

Nutty Cream Cheese Frosting: In a large bowl beat two 3-ounce packages *cream cheese,* ½ cup softened *margarine or butter,* and 2 teaspoons *vanilla* with an electric mixer on medium to high speed till light and fluffy. Gradually add 4½ to 4¾ cups sifted powdered sugar, beating to spreading consistency. Stir in ½ cup chopped *walnuts.*

*Note: For sour milk, place 1½ teaspoons lemon juice or vinegar in a measuring cup. Add enough whole milk to equal ½ cup. Makes enough for cake and Buttermilk Glaze.

Nutrition facts per serving: 728 calories, 33 g total fat (8 g saturated fat), 69 mg cholesterol, 466 mg sodium, 105 g carbohydrate, 2 g fiber, 8 g protein.
Daily Value: 80% vitamin A, 3% vitamin C, 5% calcium, and 13% iron.

RASPBERRY MOUSSE CAKE

Celebrate the summer season by serving this regal dessert when raspberries are plentiful.

1	cup all-purpose flour
2	tablespoons cornstarch
1¼	teaspoons baking powder
¼	teaspoon salt
4	egg yolks
½	cup granulated sugar
3	tablespoons water
1	teaspoon lemon juice
4	egg whites
½	cup granulated sugar
2	cups frozen red raspberries, thawed
¼	cup granulated sugar
¼	cup orange juice or orange-flavored liqueur
1	envelope unflavored gelatin
3	cups whipping cream
3	tablespoons granulated sugar
3	cups fresh red raspberries

Grease and lightly flour two 9x1½-inch round baking pans. Stir together the flour, cornstarch, baking powder, and salt. Set aside.

Beat egg yolks with an electric mixer on high speed about 5 minutes or till thick and lemon-colored. Add ½ cup sugar, water, and lemon juice, beating on low speed till combined. Thoroughly wash beaters.

Beat whites on medium to high speed till soft peaks form (tips curl). Gradually add ½ cup sugar, *2 tablespoons* at a time, beating till stiff peaks form (tips stand straight). Fold yolk mixture into white mixture. Fold flour mixture into egg mixture. Pour into prepared pans.

Bake in a 325° oven for 25 to 35 minutes or till tops spring back when lightly touched. Immediately remove from pans; cool completely on wire racks. Slice each layer in half horizontally.

Place thawed berries in a blender container. Cover; blend till smooth. Strain to remove seeds. Stir in ¼ cup sugar. Set aside. In a 1-cup glass measuring cup combine orange juice and gelatin; let stand 5 minutes. Place cup in a saucepan filled with 1 inch boiling water. Heat and stir till gelatin dissolves. Beat whipping cream and 3 tablespoons sugar on medium to high speed till soft peaks form. Gradually add gelatin mixture beating till stiff peaks form. Set aside *3½ cups* of the whipped cream mixture. Fold berry purée and *2 cups* of the fresh berries into remaining whipped cream mixture. Spread berry mixture over tops of 3 cake layers. Stack layers; top with remaining layer. Frost cake with reserved whipped cream mixture. Cover; chill 6 hours or overnight before serving. Top with remaining berries. Makes 12 servings.

Nutrition facts per serving: 393 calories, 24 g total fat (14 g saturated fat), 153 mg cholesterol, 127 mg sodium, 41 g carbohydrate, 3 g fiber, 5 g protein.
Daily Value: 37% vitamin A, 27% vitamin C, 8% calcium, 7% iron.

CARAMEL-TOPPED NUT TORTE

A food processor makes short work of mixing the batter for this rich torte. The no-fuss frosting is made with just two ingredients—cream cheese and caramel ice cream topping.

2   tablespoons all-purpose flour
1   teaspoon baking powder
½   teaspoon ground cinnamon
⅛   teaspoon salt
4   eggs
¾   cup granulated sugar
2½ cups walnuts or pecans
    Caramel-Cream Cheese
    Chopped walnuts or pecans (optional)
    Caramel ice cream topping (optional)
    Orange peel twist (optional)

Grease and lightly flour two 8x1½-inch round baking pans. Stir together flour, baking powder, cinnamon, and salt. Set aside.

In a food processor bowl place eggs and sugar. Cover and process till smooth. Add 2½ cups walnuts or pecans. Process about 1 minute or till nearly smooth. Add flour mixture; process just till combined. Pour batter into prepared pans.

Bake in a 350° oven about 20 minutes or till lightly browned. Cool in pans on wire racks 10 minutes. Remove from pans; cool completely on racks. Frost tops of layers with Caramel-Cream Cheese; stack layers. Drizzle cake with caramel ice cream topping and sprinkle with chopped walnuts or pecans, if desired. Garnish with orange peel twist, if desired. Makes 12 servings.

Caramel-Cream Cheese: Beat together two 3-ounce packages *cream cheese* and ⅓ cup *caramel ice cream topping* till fluffy.

Nutrition facts per serving: 311 calories, 22 g total fat (5 g saturated fat), 87 mg cholesterol, 150 mg sodium, 25 g carbohydrate, 1 g fiber, 7 g protein.
Daily Value: 9% vitamin A, 1% vitamin C, 6% calcium, 7% iron.

ICE CREAM CAKE

Personalize this four-layer cake by varying the flavors of ice cream, frozen yogurt, or sherbet, and by using food coloring to tint the whipped cream frosting your favorite hue.

2 cups all-purpose flour
3 teaspoons baking powder
¾ teaspoon salt
¾ cup shortening
1½ cups granulated sugar
2 teaspoons vanilla
1 cup milk
5 egg whites
1 pint chocolate ice cream or frozen yogurt, softened
1 pint mint chocolate chip or pistachio ice cream, softened
1 pint strawberry ice cream or frozen yogurt, or raspberry sherbet, softened
Green Whipped Cream
Edible flowers (optional)

Grease and lightly flour two 9x1½-inch round baking pans. Combine flour, baking powder, and salt. Set aside.

In a large mixing bowl beat shortening with an electric mixer on medium to high speed till softened. Add sugar and vanilla; beat till mixed. Alternately add flour mixture and milk, beating on low to medium speed after each addition just till mixed. Wash beaters.

In another large mixing bowl beat egg whites on medium to high speed till stiff peaks form (tips stand straight). Gently fold egg whites into flour mixture. Pour batter into prepared pans.

Bake in a 350° oven for 25 to 30 minutes or till a wooden toothpick inserted in centers comes out clean. Cool in pans on wire racks 10 minutes. Remove from pans; cool completely on wire racks. Slice each layer in half horizontally with a sharp, long-bladed knife. Spread one layer with chocolate ice cream or frozen yogurt; top with second layer. Spread with mint chocolate chip or pistachio ice cream; top with third layer. Spread with strawberry ice cream or raspberry sherbet; top with remaining layer. Freeze 12 to 24 hours. Frost cake with Green Whipped Cream. Freeze at least 30 minutes or till frosting is firm before serving. Store cake, covered, in freezer. Before serving, garnish with edible flowers, if desired. Makes 12 to 16 servings.

Green Whipped Cream: In a chilled small mixing bowl, beat 1½ cups *whipping cream,* 3 tablespoons *granulated sugar,* ½ teaspoon *vanilla,* and 1 to 2 drops *green food coloring* with an electric mixer on medium to high speed till soft peaks form.

Nutrition facts per serving: 527 calories, 30 g total fat (14 g saturated fat), 59 mg cholesterol, 304 mg sodium, 61 g carbohydrate, 1 g fiber, 7 g protein.
Daily Value: 19% vitamin A, 6% vitamin C, 16% calcium, 8% iron.

VANILLA RASPBERRY TORTE

Pretty ribbons of raspberry preserves separate layers of tender golden yellow cake in this vanilla-frosted torte.

2   cups all-purpose flour
2   teaspoons baking powder
½   teaspoon salt
½   cup margarine or butter
1¼ cups granulated sugar
2   teaspoons vanilla
2   eggs
¾   cup milk
¾   cup raspberry preserves
     Vanilla Butter Frosting (see recipe,
        page 42)
     Raspberry preserves (optional)
     Fresh raspberries (optional)

Grease and lightly flour two 9x1½-inch round baking pans. Combine flour, baking powder, and salt. Set aside.

In a large mixing bowl beat margarine or butter with an electric mixer on medium to high speed for 30 seconds or till softened. Add sugar and vanilla; beat till combined. Add eggs, one at a time, beating well after each. Alternately add flour mixture and milk, beating on low to medium speed after each addition just till combined. Pour batter into the prepared pans.

Bake in a 350° oven for 20 to 25 minutes or till a wooden toothpick inserted in centers comes out clean. Cool in pans on wire racks 10 minutes. Remove from pans. Cool completely on wire racks. Split cake layers in half horizontally with a sharp, long-bladed knife.

Spread *each* of *three* layers with ¼ *cup* of the raspberry preserves. Stack the layers; top with the remaining cake layer. Frost the sides and top of cake with Vanilla Butter Frosting. Drizzle with additional raspberry preserves and top with fresh raspberries, if desired. Makes 12 to 16 servings.

Nutrition facts per serving: 490 calories, 14 g total fat (3 g saturated fat), 37 mg cholesterol, 322 mg sodium, 89 g carbohydrate, 1 g fiber, 4 g protein.
Daily Value: 18% vitamin A, 0% vitamin C, 8% calcium, 9% iron.

LEMON CRYSTAL CUPCAKES

A mixture of fresh lemon juice and sugar gives these little gems a crystally coating.

2   cups all-purpose flour
2½   teaspoons baking powder
¼   teaspoon salt
⅔   cup shortening
1   cup granulated sugar
⅔   cup milk
3   eggs
1   tablespoon finely shredded lemon peel
⅔   cup granulated sugar
⅓   cup lemon juice
     Crystal sugar (optional)
     Violets (optional)

Grease and lightly flour twenty 2½-inch muffin cups. Stir together flour, baking powder, and salt.

In a large mixing bowl beat shortening with an electric mixer on medium to high speed for 30 seconds or till softened. Add 1 cup sugar; beat till combined. Add eggs, one at a time, beating well after each addition. Alternately add flour mixture and milk, beating on low to medium speed after each addition just till combined. Stir in lemon peel. Pour batter into prepared muffin cups. Fill any remaining muffin cups with water to avoid damaging pan.

Bake in a 350° oven for 20 to 25 minutes or till a wooden toothpick inserted in centers comes out clean. Cool in pans on wire racks for 5 minutes. Remove from pans. Place cupcakes upside-down on wire racks set over waxed paper.

In a small mixing bowl stir together ⅔ cups sugar and lemon juice. Brush sugar mixture over warm cupcakes till all is absorbed. Cool completely. Sprinkle with crystal sugar and top with violets, if desired. Makes 20 cupcakes.

Nutrition information per cupcake: 184 calories, 8 g total fat (2 g saturated fat), 33 mg cholesterol, 86 mg sodium, 26 g carbohydrate, 0 g fiber, 2 g protein.
Daily Value: 1% vitamin A, 3% vitamin C, 4% calcium, 4% iron.

RAINBOW CUPCAKES

From one frosting, you make six different flavors—vanilla, lemon, coffee, chocolate, maple, and raspberry.

2   cups all-purpose flour
1½ teaspoons baking powder
¼   teaspoon salt
⅔   cup margarine or butter
1¼ cups granulated sugar
1   teaspoon vanilla
2   eggs
1   cup milk
    Butter Cream Frosting
    Multicolored nonpareils
1   teaspoon lemon juice
¼   teaspoon finely shredded lemon peel
1   drop yellow food coloring
    Flaked coconut
¼   teaspoon instant coffee crystals
½   teaspoon hot water
    Chocolate sprinkles
1   tablespoon unsweetened cocoa
      powder
    Colored chocolate sprinkles
¼   teaspoon maple flavoring
    Chopped walnuts
½   teaspoon raspberry flavoring or 4 to 6
      drops peppermint extract
1   drop red food coloring
    Multicolored coarse sugar

Grease and lightly flour twenty-four 2½-inch muffin cups or line with paper bake cups. Stir together all-purpose flour, baking powder, and salt. Beat margarine or butter with an electric mixer on medium to high speed till softened. Add sugar and vanilla; beat till combined. Add eggs, one at a time, beating well after each. Alternately add flour mixture and milk, beating on low to medium speed after each addition just till mixed. Pour into the prepared muffin cups. Bake in a 350° oven for 20 to 25 minutes or till a toothpick inserted in centers comes out clean. Cool in pans 5 minutes. Remove from pans. Cool completely on wire rack.

Divide Butter Cream Frosting into 6 equal portions. Frost *4* cupcakes with first portion; sprinkle with multicolored nonpareils. To second portion, stir in lemon juice, lemon peel, and yellow food coloring, adding a little additional powdered sugar, if necessary. Frost *4* cupcakes; sprinkle with coconut. Dissolve coffee crystals in hot water; add to third portion. Frost *4* cupcakes; top with chocolate sprinkles. To fourth portion, stir in cocoa powder, adding a little additional milk, if necessary. Frost *4* cup cakes; sprinkle with colored chocolate sprinkles. To fifth portion, stir in maple flavoring. Frost *4* cupcakes; sprinkle with walnuts. To the last portion, stir in raspberry flavoring or peppermint extract and red food coloring. Frost remaining *4* cupcakes. Sprinkle with multicolored coarse sugar. Makes 24 cupcakes.

Butter Cream Frosting: Beat ½ cup *margarine or butter* and 1 teaspoon *vanilla* till fluffy. Gradually add 4 cups *sifted powdered sugar* alternately with ¼ cup *milk* beating well after each addition. Beat in additional milk, if necessary, to make of spreading consistency.

Nutrition information per cupcake: 241 calories, 10 g total fat (2 g saturated fat), 19 mg cholesterol, 161 mg sodium, 38 g carbohydrate, 0 g fiber, 2 g protein.
Daily Value: 12% vitamin A, 0% vitamin C, 3% calcium, and 3% iron.

CAKELETS À L'ORANGE

These tender, light cupcakes made from a sponge cake batter can be baked in advance and frozen. But wait to brush them with the warmed marmalade till just before serving.

1   cup all-purpose flour
1   teaspoon baking powder
¼   teaspoon salt
2   eggs
1   cup granulated sugar
2   teaspoons finely shredded orange peel
½   cup milk
2   tablespoons margarine or butter
½   cup orange marmalade
1   tablespoon orange juice
    Sweetened Whipped Cream (optional)
      (see recipe, page 22)
    Orange peel strips (optional)

Grease and lightly flour eighteen 2½-inch muffin cups. Combine flour, baking powder, and salt. Set aside.

In a small mixing bowl beat the eggs with an electric mixer on high speed about 4 minutes or till thick and lemon-colored. Gradually add the sugar, about *2 tablespoons* at a time, beating on medium speed for 4 to 5 minutes or till sugar is almost dissolved. Add flour mixture and 2 teaspoons orange peel to egg mixture, beating on low to medium speed just till combined.

In a small saucepan heat milk and margarine or butter over medium heat till margarine or butter is melted. Stir milk mixture into batter till well combined. Pour batter into prepared muffin cups.

Bake in a 350° oven for 15 to 18 minutes or till tops spring back when lightly touched. Cool in pans on wire racks for 5 minutes. Remove from pans. Cool completely on wire racks.

In a small saucepan cook and stir orange marmalade and orange juice over low heat till melted; brush over cupcakes. If desired, serve with Sweetened Whipped Cream and garnish with orange peel strips. Makes 18 cupcakes.

Nutrition facts per serving: 113 calories, 2 g total fat (1 g saturated fat), 24 mg cholesterol, 77 mg sodium, 23 g carbohydrate, 1 g fiber, 2 g protein.
Daily Value: 3% vitamin A, 2% vitamin C, 2% calcium, 3% iron.

CHOCOLATE FUDGE CAKE

Sour cream makes this chocolate cake moist and tender. Pipe a decorative border, add a special greeting, and top with some candles for the ultimate birthday cake.

1¾ cups all-purpose flour
1 teaspoon baking soda
½ teaspoon salt
½ cup shortening
1½ cups granulated sugar
½ teaspoon vanilla
2 eggs
3 ounces unsweetened chocolate, melted and cooled
½ cup dairy sour cream
1 cup cold water
Sour Cream-Fudge Frosting

Grease and lightly flour two 8x1½-inch or 9x1½-inch round baking pans. Combine flour, baking soda, and salt. Set aside.

In a large mixing bowl beat shortening with an electric mixer on medium to high speed about 30 seconds or till softened. Add sugar and vanilla; beat till combined. Add eggs, one at a time, beating well after each. Beat in cooled chocolate and sour cream. Alternately add flour mixture and cold water, beating on low to medium speed after each addition just till combined. Pour batter into prepared pans.

Bake in a 350° oven for 25 to 30 minutes or till a wooden toothpick inserted in centers comes out clean. Cool in pans on wire racks 10 minutes. Remove from pans. Cool completely on wire racks. Fill and frost cake with Sour Cream-Fudge Frosting. Store in refrigerator. Makes 12 servings.

Sour Cream-Fudge Frosting: In a medium saucepan melt 3 ounces *unsweetened chocolate* and ⅓ cup *margarine or butter* over low heat. Remove from heat; cool. Stir in ½ cup *dairy sour cream* and 1 teaspoon *vanilla*. Gradually add 3 cups sifted *powdered sugar*, beating till smooth and of spreading consistency.

Nutrition facts per serving: 500 calories, 26 g total fat (9 g saturated fat), 44 mg cholesterol, 276 mg sodium, 68 g carbohydrate, 1 g fiber, 5 g protein.
Daily Value: 12% vitamin A, 0% vitamin C, 3% calcium, 12% iron.

CHOCOLATE CREAM CAKE

This trio of devil's food layers is first filled with vanilla butter cream and then the entire cake is swirled with chocolatey cream cheese frosting—an irresistible combination!

2⅔ cups all-purpose flour
1½ teaspoons baking soda
¾ teaspoon salt
¾ cup margarine or butter
2¼ cups granulated sugar
2 teaspoons vanilla
3 eggs
3 ounces unsweetened chocolate, melted and cooled
1½ cups ice water
    Butter Cream Filling
    Chocolate-Cream Cheese Frosting

Grease and lightly flour three 9x1½-inch or 8x1½-inch baking pans. Combine flour, baking soda, and salt. Set aside.

In a large mixing bowl beat margarine or butter with an electric mixer on medium to high speed about 30 seconds or till softened. Add sugar and vanilla; beat till combined. Add eggs, one at a time, beating well after each. Beat in cooled chocolate. Alternately add flour mixture and ice water, beating on low to medium speed after each addition just till combined. Pour batter into prepared pans.

Bake in a 350° oven for 25 to 30 minutes or till a wooden toothpick inserted in centers comes out clean. Cool in pans on wire racks for 10 minutes. Remove from pans. Cool completely on wire racks. Spread Butter Cream Filling on *two* of the layers; stack layers. Top with remaining layer. Frost cake with Chocolate Cream-Cheese Frosting. Store in refrigerator. Makes 12 servings.

Butter Cream Filling: Beat ½ cup *margarine or butter* with an electric mixer on medium to high speed till softened. Beat in 2¼ cups sifted *powdered sugar,* 2 tablespoons *milk,* and ½ teaspoon *vanilla.* Beat in additional milk, if necessary, to make of spreading consistency.

Chocolate-Cream Cheese Frosting: Beat ½ of an 8-ounce package *cream cheese* with an electric mixer on medium to high speed till softened. Beat in 3 tablespoons *milk* till smooth. Gradually add 3¾ cups sifted *powdered sugar,* beating well. Beat in 3 ounces *unsweetened chocolate,* melted and cooled, and 1 teaspoon *vanilla.* Beat in additional milk, if necessary, to make frosting of spreading consistency.

Nutrition facts per serving: 730 calories, 32 g total fat (9 g saturated fat), 64 mg cholesterol, 564 mg sodium, 113 g carbohydrate, 2 g fiber, 7 g protein.
Daily Value: 30% vitamin A, 0% vitamin C, 3% calcium, 17% iron.

CHOCOLATE-RASPBERRY CAKE

A cloud of fluffy frosting, tinted pink with raspberry preserves, adorns these light chocolate layers.

1½ cups all-purpose flour
1 cup granulated sugar
1 teaspoon baking powder
½ teaspoon baking soda
½ teaspoon salt
1 cup buttermilk or sour milk*
⅓ cup cooking oil
2 egg yolks
2 ounces unsweetened chocolate, melted and cooled
2 egg whites
½ cup granulated sugar
3 tablespoons raspberry liqueur
   Fluffy Raspberry Frosting

Grease and lightly flour two 9x1½-inch round baking pans. Set aside.

In a large bowl mix flour, 1 cup sugar, baking powder, soda, and salt. Make a well in center of flour mixture. Add buttermilk, oil, yolks, and chocolate. Beat with an electric mixer on low to medium speed till mixed. Beat on medium to high speed till smooth. Wash beaters. In a medium bowl beat egg whites on medium to high speed till soft peaks form (tips curl). Add ½ cup sugar, *2 tablespoons* at a time, beating on medium to high speed till stiff peaks form (tips stand straight). Fold into chocolate mixture. Pour into prepared pans.

Bake in a 350° oven for 25 to 30 minutes or till tops spring back when lightly touched. Cool in pans on wire racks 10 minutes. Remove from pans. Cool completely on racks. Brush layers with liqueur. Fill and frost cake with Fluffy Raspberry Frosting. Serves 12.

Fluffy Raspberry Frosting: Melt ⅓ cup seedless *raspberry preserves;* keep warm. In top of double boiler combine 1½ cups *granulated sugar,* ⅓ cup *cold water,* 2 *egg whites,* and ¼ teaspoon *cream of tartar* or 2 teaspoons *light corn syrup.* Beat with electric mixer on low speed for 30 seconds. Place over boiling water (upper pan should not touch water). Cook, beating constantly with electric mixer on high speed for 7 to 9 minutes or till stiff peaks forms (tips stand straight). Beat in preserves and, if desired, 1 or 2 drops *red food coloring.* Remove from the heat. Beat 2 to 3 minutes more or till spreading consistency.

*Note: For sour milk, place 1 tablespoon lemon juice or vinegar in a measuring cup. Add enough whole milk to equal 1 cup.

Nutrition facts per serving: 381 calories, 10 g total fat (2 g saturated fat), 36 mg cholesterol, 215 mg sodium, 71 g carbohydrate, 1 g fiber, 4 g protein.
Daily Value: 5% vitamin A, 0% vitamin C, 5% calcium, 8% iron.

GERMAN CHOCOLATE CAKE

Sweet chocolate gives this cake a delicate flavor enhanced by the coconut and pecan frosting.

1 4-ounce package German sweet
    chocolate
⅓ cup water
1⅔ cups all-purpose flour
1 teaspoon baking soda
½ teaspoon salt
½ cup margarine or butter
1 cup granulated sugar
1 teaspoon vanilla
3 egg yolks
⅔ cup buttermilk or sour milk*
3 egg whites
    Coconut-Pecan Frosting

Grease and lightly flour two 8x1½-inch or 9x1½-inch round baking pans. In a small saucepan heat chocolate and water over low heat till chocolate is melted; cool. Combine flour, soda, and salt. Set aside.

In a large mixing bowl beat margarine or butter with an electric mixer on medium to high speed till softened. Add sugar and vanilla; beat till combined. Add egg yolks, one at a time, beating well after each. Beat in chocolate mixture. Alternately add flour mixture and buttermilk or sour milk, beating on low to medium speed after each addition just till combined. Thoroughly wash beaters.

In a medium bowl beat egg whites on high speed till stiff peaks form (tips stand straight). Fold whites into batter. Pour into prepared pans.

Bake in a 350° oven for 30 to 35 minutes for 8-inch layers or 20 to 25 minutes for 9-inch layers. Cool in pans or wire racks 10 minutes. Remove from pans. Cool completely on racks. Spread Coconut-Pecan Frosting on top of each layer; stack layers. Store cake in refrigerator. Makes 12 servings.

Coconut-Pecan Frosting: In a medium saucepan mix ⅔ cup *granulated sugar* and 1 *egg*. Add one 5⅓-ounce can (⅔ cup) *evaporated milk*, ¼ cup *margarine or butter*, and dash *salt*. Cook and stir over medium heat about 12 minutes or till thick and bubbly. Stir in one 3½-ounce can (1⅓ cups) flaked *coconut* and ½ cup chopped *pecans*. Cool.

Note: For sour milk, place 2 teaspoons lemon juice or vinegar in a measuring cup. Add enough whole milk to equal ⅔ cup.

Nutrition facts per serving: 432 calories, 23 g total fat (8 g saturated fat), 76 mg cholesterol, 392 mg sodium, 52 g carbohydrate, 2 g fiber, 6 g protein.
Daily Value: 24% vitamin A, 0% vitamin C, 6% calcium, 9% iron.

SOUR CREAM COCOA CAKE

This moist cocoa cake is so rich that you can skip frosting it—just a sprinkling of powdered sugar will do. For a lovely stenciled effect, place a paper doily on the cake. Sift powdered sugar over the cake, then carefully remove the doily.

1¾ cups all-purpose flour
½ cup unsweetened cocoa powder
1 teaspoon baking powder
½ teaspoon baking soda
½ teaspoon salt
¾ cup shortening
1½ cups granulated sugar
½ teaspoon vanilla
2 eggs
½ cup dairy sour cream
1 cup cold water
Sifted powdered sugar (optional)

Grease and lightly flour a 9-inch springform pan. Combine flour, cocoa powder, baking powder, baking soda, and salt.

In a mixing bowl beat shortening with an electric mixer on medium to high speed about 30 seconds or till softened. Add sugar and vanilla; beat till combined. Add eggs, one at a time, beating well after each. Stir in sour cream. Alternately add flour mixture and cold water, beating on low to medium speed after each addition just till combined. Pour into prepared pan.

Bake in a 350° oven about 1¼ hours or till a wooden toothpick inserted in center comes out clean. Cool in pan on wire rack for 10 minutes. Remove from pan. Cool completely on wire rack. If desired, sift powdered sugar over cake top. Makes 16 servings.

Nutrition facts per serving: 240 calories, 12 g total fat (4 g saturated fat), 30 mg cholesterol, 141 mg sodium, 30 g carbohydrate, 0 g fiber, 3 g protein.
Daily Value: 2% vitamin A, 0% vitamin C, 5% calcium, 7% iron.

GRASSHOPPER CAKE

This deep, dark, chocolate beauty is filled and frosted with a minty marshmallow cream.

2¼ cups all-purpose flour
1¾ cups granulated sugar
⅔ cup unsweetened cocoa powder
1½ teaspoons baking powder
1 teaspoon baking soda
½ teaspoon salt
1½ cups water
¾ cup cooking oil
2 eggs
1½ teaspoons vanilla
    Marshmallow-Mint Cream
    Layered chocolate mint candies
        (optional)

Grease and lightly flour two 9x1½-inch baking pans. Set aside.

In a large mixing bowl mix flour, sugar, cocoa powder, baking powder, baking soda, and salt. Add water, oil, eggs, and vanilla. Beat with an electric mixer on low to medium speed till combined. Beat for 2 minutes on medium to high speed. Pour batter into prepared pans.

Bake in a 350° oven for 30 to 35 minutes or till a wooden toothpick inserted in centers comes out clean. Cool in pans on wire racks for 10 minutes. Remove from pans. Cool completely on wire racks. Up to 1 hour before serving, fill and frost cake with Marshmallow-Mint Cream. Store frosted cake in refrigerator. If desired, use a vegetable peeler to cut curls from the layered chocolate mint candies. Sprinkle candy curls over top of cake. Makes 12 servings.

Marshmallow-Mint Cream: In small mixing bowl place one 7-ounce jar *marshmallow creme;* gradually beat in ¼ cup *green creme de menthe* with an electric mixer on low speed till smooth. In a chilled small mixing bowl beat 1½ cups *whipping cream* on medium to high speed till soft peaks form. Gently fold marshmallow mixture into whipped cream. If necessary, beat just till mixture mounds.

Nutrition facts per serving: 521 calories, 26 g total fat (9 g saturated fat), 76 mg cholesterol, 270 mg sodium, 64 g carbohydrate, 1 g fiber, 5 g protein.
Daily Value: 14% vitamin A, 0% vitamin C, 10% calcium, 12% iron.

CHOCOLATE CINNAMON CAKE

This extra-chocolatey spice cake calls for a cup of strong coffee. If you haven't any brewed on hand, just make a cup with instant coffee crystals.

1¾ cups all-purpose flour
2 teaspoons baking soda
1½ teaspoons ground cinnamon
⅛ teaspoon ground cloves
½ cup margarine or butter
1 cup granulated sugar
1 teaspoon vanilla
2 eggs
4 ounces unsweetened chocolate, melted and cooled
1 cup cold strong coffee
Cinnamon Whipped Cream
½ cup chopped pecans or walnuts
Whole pecans or walnut halves (optional)

Grease and lightly flour two 8x1½-inch or 9x1½-inch round baking pans. Combine flour, baking soda, cinnamon, and cloves. Set aside.

In a large mixing bowl beat margarine or butter with an electric mixer on medium to high speed about 30 seconds or till softened. Add sugar and vanilla; beat till combined. Add eggs, one at a time, beating well after each. Stir in cooled chocolate. Alternately add flour mixture and cold coffee, beating on low to medium speed after each addition just till combined. Pour batter into prepared pans.

Bake in a 350° oven for 25 to 30 minutes or till a wooden toothpick inserted in the centers comes out clean. Cool in pans on wire racks for 10 minutes. Remove from pans. Cool completely on wire racks.

Stir together ½ *cup* of the Cinnamon Whipped Cream and chopped pecans or walnuts. Spread over one cake layer. Top with remaining cake layer. Frost top and sides of cake with remaining Cinnamon Whipped Cream. Store frosted cake in the refrigerator. If desired, top with whole pecans or walnut halves. Makes 12 servings.

Cinnamon Whipped Cream: In a chilled large mixing bowl beat 2 cups *whipping cream,* ¼ cup *granulated sugar,* 2 teaspoons *vanilla,* and ½ teaspoon ground *cinnamon* with an electric mixer on medium to high speed till soft peaks form.

Nutrition facts per serving: 443 calories, 31 g total fat (13 g saturated fat), 90 mg cholesterol, 326 mg sodium, 40 g carbohydrate, 1 g fiber, 5 g protein.
Daily Value: 28% vitamin A, 0% vitamin C, 4% calcium, 12% iron.

DOUBLE FUDGE CAKE

Served right from the pan, this fudgy cocoa cake topped with an even fudgier chocolate frosting, is sure to be a hit at picnics, potlucks, and any other event that calls for casual dining.

2¼ cups all-purpose flour
½ cup unsweetened cocoa powder
1½ teaspoons baking soda
1 teaspoon salt
½ cup shortening
1 cup granulated sugar
1 teaspoon vanilla
3 egg yolks
1⅓ cups cold water
3 egg whites
¾ cup granulated sugar
   Fudge Frosting

Grease a 13x9x2-inch baking pan. Combine flour, cocoa powder, baking soda, and salt. Set aside.

In a large mixing bowl beat shortening with an electric mixer on medium speed about 30 seconds or till softened. Add 1 cup sugar and vanilla; beat till combined. Add egg yolks, one at a time, beating well after each. Alternately add flour mixture and water, beating on low to medium speed after each addition just till combined. Thoroughly wash beaters.

In a large mixing bowl beat egg whites on medium to high speed till soft peaks form (tips curl). Gradually add ¾ cup sugar, about *2 tablespoons* at a time, beating till stiff peaks form (tips stand straight). Fold *2 cups* of the cocoa batter into the egg white mixture to lighten. Gently fold cocoa-egg white mixture back into remaining batter till combined. Pour batter into prepared pan.

Bake in a 350° oven about 40 minutes or till a wooden toothpick inserted in center comes out clean. Cool completely in pan on wire rack. Frost with Fudge Frosting. Makes 12 servings.

Fudge Frosting: In a medium saucepan combine one 5-ounce can *evaporated milk,* ½ cup *granulated sugar,* and 2 tablespoons *margarine or butter.* Cook and stir over medium heat till mixture is boiling; boil 5 minutes, stirring occasionally. Remove from heat; add 1½ cups *semisweet chocolate pieces,* stirring till melted. Add 1 tablespoon *light corn syrup;* stir till mixed. Use immediately.

Nutrition facts per serving: 471 calories, 19 g total fat (3 g saturated fat), 57 mg cholesterol, 389 mg sodium, 72 g carbohydrate, 1 g fiber, 7 g protein.
Daily Value: 11% vitamin A, 0% vitamin C, 7% calcium, 15% iron.

CHOCOLATE POUND CAKE

A dollop of almond-scented whipped cream makes the perfect foil for this large, handsome, deliciously dark chocolate cake.

4 cups all-purpose flour
3 cups granulated sugar
1 tablespoon baking powder
1½ teaspoons baking soda
½ teaspoon salt
2½ cups milk
1½ cups butter, softened
8 ounces unsweetened chocolate, melted and cooled
5 eggs
1 teaspoon vanilla
½ teaspoon almond extract
Almond Whipped Cream
Toasted sliced almonds (optional)

Grease and lightly flour a 10-inch tube pan. Set aside.

In an extra-large mixing bowl combine flour, sugar, baking powder, baking soda, and salt. Add milk, butter, and cooled chocolate. Beat with an electric mixer on low to medium speed till combined. Beat on medium speed 2 minutes. Add eggs, vanilla, and almond extract. Beat 2 minutes more. Pour batter into the prepared pan, spreading evenly. Use a knife to cut a zigzag pattern through batter to break up any large air bubbles.

Bake in a 325° for 1½ to 1¾ hours or till a wooden toothpick inserted in center comes out clean. Cool in pan on a wire rack 20 minutes. Remove cake from pan. Cool completely on wire rack. Serve slices with Almond Whipped Cream. If desired, sprinkle with toasted almonds. Makes 16 to 20 servings.

Almond Whipped Cream: In a chilled medium mixing bowl combine 1 cup *whipping cream*, 2 tablespoons *granulated sugar*, and ¼ teaspoon *almond extract* or 1 teaspoon *amaretto*. Beat with an electric mixer on medium to high speed till soft peaks form.

Nutrition facts per serving: 572 calories, 33 g total fat (18g saturated fat), 136 mg cholesterol, 473 mg sodium, 68 g carbohydrate, 2 g fiber, 8 g protein.
Daily Value: 27% vitamin A, 0% vitamin C, 12% calcium, 18% iron.

COFFEE-TOFFEE TOPPED CHOCOLATE ANGEL FOOD CAKE

Coffee and chocolate flavors team up to create this elegant dessert. A sprinkle of crushed candy bars becomes a crunchy toffee topping.

1½ cups egg whites (11 to 12 large)
1½ cups sifted powdered sugar
 1   cup sifted cake flour or ⅔ cup sifted
       all-purpose flour
 ¼   cup unsweetened cocoa powder
1½ teaspoons cream of tartar
 1   teaspoon vanilla
 1   cup granulated sugar
       Coffee Cream
 2   1.4-ounce chocolate-covered toffee
       candy bars, crushed

In a very large mixing bowl allow egg whites to stand at room temperature for 30 minutes. Meanwhile, sift together powdered sugar, cake flour or all-purpose flour, and cocoa powder 3 times; set aside.

Add cream of tartar and vanilla to egg whites. Beat with an electric mixer on medium to high speed till soft peaks form (tips curl). Gradually add sugar, about *2 tablespoons* at a time, beating till stiff peaks form (tips stand straight).

Sift about *one-fourth* of the flour mixture over egg white mixture; fold in gently. (If bowl is too full, transfer to larger bowl.) Repeat with remaining flour mixture, using about one-fourth of the flour mixture each time. Spoon batter into an ungreased 10-inch tube pan. Gently cut through batter with a knife or narrow metal spatula to remove any large air pockets.

Bake on the lowest rack in a 350° oven for 40 to 45 minutes or till top springs back when lightly touched. Immediately invert cake in pan; cool completely. Loosen sides of cake from pan; remove cake. Place cake upside down on plate; frost with Coffee Cream. Sprinkle with crushed candy. Store, covered, in the refrigerator. Serves 12.

Coffee Cream: In a medium mixing bowl dissolve 2 teaspoons *instant coffee crystals* in 1 tablespoon *hot water;* add one 7-ounce jar *marshmallow creme* and ½ teaspoon *vanilla*. Beat with an electric mixer on medium to high speed till smooth. In a chilled small mixing bowl beat 1 cup *whipping cream* on medium to high speed till stiff peaks form. Gently fold whipped cream into marshmallow mixture.

Nutrition facts per serving: 325 calories, 10 g total fat (5 g saturated fat), 29 mg cholesterol, 87 mg sodium, 55 g carbohydrate, 0 g fiber, 5 g protein.
Daily Value: 9% vitamin A, 0% vitamin C, 3% calcium, 6% iron.

MOCHA CHIFFON LOAF WITH MOCHA ICING

For a winning combination and double the mocha taste, we've blended coffee and chocolate flavors in both the cake and the glaze!

⅓   cup water
2   ounces unsweetened chocolate
2   tablespoons granulated sugar
1½ teaspoons instant coffee crystals
1   cup plus 2 tablespoons sifted
      cake flour or 1 cup sifted all-
      purpose flour
¾   cup granulated sugar
1½ teaspoons baking powder
¼   teaspoon salt
⅓   cup cold water
⅓   cup cooking oil
4   egg yolks
½   teaspoon vanilla
4   egg whites
½   teaspoon cream of tartar
      Mocha Icing

In a small saucepan combine the ⅓ cup water, chocolate, 2 table-spoons sugar, and coffee crystals. Heat and stir over low heat till chocolate melts; set aside to cool.

Meanwhile, in a large mixing bowl combine flour, ¾ cup sugar, baking powder, and salt. Make a well in the center of flour mixture. Add the ⅓ cup cold water, oil, egg yolks, and vanilla. Beat with an electric mixer on low to medium speed till combined. Beat on high speed about 1 minute or till smooth. Fold in cooled chocolate mixture. Thoroughly wash beaters.

In a very large bowl beat egg whites and cream of tartar on medium to high speed till stiff peaks form (tips stand straight). Pour beaten mixture in a thin stream over egg white mixture, folding in gently just till combined. Pour into an ungreased 9x5x3-inch loaf pan.

Bake in a 325° oven for 55 to 60 minutes or till top springs back when lightly touched. Immediately invert cake in pan; cool completely. Loosen sides of cake from pan; remove. Drizzle with Mocha Icing. Makes 12 servings.

Mocha Icing: In a small mixing bowl dissolve 1 teaspoon *instant coffee crystals* in 1 tablespoon *hot water.* Add ¾ cup sifted *powdered sugar,* 1 tablespoon *unsweetened cocoa powder,* and 1 tablespoon melted *margarine or butter.* Stir in additional powdered sugar or water to make icing of a drizzling consistency.

Nutrition facts per serving: 232 calories, 11 g total fat (3 g saturated fat), 71 mg cholesterol, 123 mg sodium, 31 g carbohydrate, 0 g fiber, 4 g protein.
Daily Value: 12% vitamin A, 0% vitamin C, 5% calcium, 8% iron.

CHOCOLATE ALMOND ICE CREAM ROLL WITH RASPBERRY SAUCE

Make this elegant dessert up to two weeks in advance and store it, tightly wrapped, in your freezer.

⅓ cup all-purpose flour
¼ cup unsweetened cocoa powder
1 teaspoon baking powder
¼ teaspoon salt
4 egg yolks
½ teaspoon vanilla
⅓ cup granulated sugar
4 egg whites
½ cup granulated sugar
 Sifted powdered sugar
1 quart butter almond or chocolate
　 almond ice cream, softened
 Raspberry Sauce
 Fresh raspberries (optional)
 Fresh mint sprigs (optional)

Grease and flour a 15x10x1-inch jelly-roll pan. Stir together flour, cocoa powder, baking powder, and salt. Set aside.

In a small mixing bowl beat egg yolks and vanilla with an electric mixer on high speed about 5 minutes or till thick and lemon-colored. Gradually add ⅓ cup sugar, beating on medium speed about 5 minutes or till sugar is almost dissolved. Thoroughly wash beaters.

In a large mixing bowl beat egg whites on medium to high speed till soft peaks form (tips curl). Gradually add the ½ cup granulated sugar, beating till stiff peaks form (tips stand straight). Fold yolk mixture into egg white mixture. Sprinkle flour mixture over egg mixture; fold in gently, just till combined. Spread batter evenly into prepared pan.

Bake in 375° oven for 12 to 15 minutes or till top springs back when lightly touched. Immediately loosen edges of cake from pan; turn out onto a towel sprinkled with sifted powdered sugar. Starting with a narrow end, roll up cake and towel together. Cool on a wire rack.

Unroll cake. Spread softened ice cream on cake to within 1 inch of edges. Reroll cake without towel. Wrap and freeze at least 4 hours before serving. To serve, drizzle Raspberry Sauce over serving plates. Slice cake and place on plates. If desired, garnish with fresh raspberries and fresh mint. Makes 10 servings.

Raspberry Sauce: In a small saucepan combine ⅔ cup *seedless raspberry preserves,* 1 tablespoon *lemon juice,* and ¼ teaspoon *almond extract.* Cook and stir just till melted. Cool slightly.

Nutrition facts per serving: 255 calories, 7 g total fat (3 g saturated fat), 116 mg cholesterol, 138 mg sodium, 44 g carbohydrate, 0 g fiber, 5 g protein.
Daily Value: 18% vitamin A, 1% vitamin C, 9% calcium, 6% iron.

CHOCOLATE-MINT CAKE ROLL

This luscious dessert roll features tender chocolate sponge cake wrapped around a cool green mint filling studded with pieces of chocolate mint candy—seconds, please!

⅔ cup all-purpose flour
⅓ cup unsweetened cocoa powder
1 teaspoon baking powder
⅛ teaspoon salt
4 eggs
¾ cup granulated sugar
¼ cup water
1 teaspoon vanilla
   Sifted powdered sugar
   Mint Cream Filling
¼ cup semisweet chocolate pieces, melted
½ teaspoon shortening

Grease and flour a 15x10x1-inch jelly-roll pan. Stir together flour, cocoa powder, baking powder, and salt. Set aside.

In large mixing bowl beat eggs, sugar, water, and vanilla with an electric mixer on high speed about 5 minutes or till thick and lemon-colored. Sprinkle flour mixture over egg mixture; fold in gently, just till combined. Spread batter evenly in prepared pan.

Bake in 375° oven for 12 to 15 minutes or till top springs back when lightly touched. Immediately loosen edges of cake from pan; turn out onto a towel sprinkled with powdered sugar. Starting with a narrow end, roll up warm cake and towel together. Cool completely on a wire rack. Unroll cake. Spread Mint Cream Filling on cake to within ½ inch of edges. Reroll cake without towel.

In a small saucepan melt chocolate pieces and shortening over low heat, stirring constantly. Drizzle over top of cake. Chill at least 2 hours before serving. Store cake in the refrigerator. Serves 10.

Mint Cream Filling: In 1-cup glass measuring cup mix 1 tablespoon *cold water* and ½ teaspoon *unflavored gelatin*. Let stand 2 minutes. Place measuring cup in saucepan of boiling water. Cook and stir 1 minute or till gelatin is completely dissolved. Set aside. In a chilled medium mixing bowl beat 1 cup *whipping cream*, 2 tablespoons *granulated sugar*, and, if desired, a few drops *green food coloring* with an electric mixer on medium to high speed while gradually drizzling the gelatin mixture over the cream mixture. Continue beating till stiff peaks form. Fold in ½ cup chopped *layered chocolate-mint candies*.

Nutrition facts per serving: 273 calories, 14 g total fat (7 g saturated fat), 118 mg cholesterol, 101 mg sodium, 32 g carbohydrate, 0 g fiber, 5 g protein.
Daily Value: 14% vitamin A, 0% vitamin C, 8% calcium, 8% iron.

MOCHA TRUFFLE ROLL

A sinfully rich and silky smooth mocha butter filling generously fills this chocolate cake roll.

⅓ cup all-purpose flour
¼ cup unsweetened cocoa powder
¼ teaspoon baking soda
¼ teaspoon salt
4 egg yolks
½ teaspoon vanilla
⅓ cup granulated sugar
4 egg whites
½ cup granulated sugar
   Sifted powdered sugar
   Mocha Truffle Filling
   Unsweetened cocoa powder

Grease and lightly flour a 15x10x1-inch jelly-roll pan. Stir together flour, ¼ cup cocoa powder, baking soda, and salt. Set aside.

In a small bowl beat egg yolks and vanilla with an electric mixer on high speed 5 minutes or till thick and lemon-colored. Gradually add ⅓ cup sugar, beating till sugar is almost dissolved. Wash beaters.

In a large bowl beat egg whites on medium to high speed till soft peaks form (tips curl). Gradually add ½ cup sugar, about *2 tablespoons* at a time, beating till stiff peaks form (tips stand straight). Fold yolk mixture into whites. Sprinkle flour mixture over egg mixture; fold in gently, just till combined. Spread batter evenly in prepared pan.

Bake in 375° oven for 12 to 15 minutes or till cake springs back when lightly touched. Immediately loosen edges of cake; turn out onto a towel sprinkled with sifted powdered sugar. Starting with a narrow end, roll up cake and towel together. Cool on a wire rack. Unroll cake. Spread Mocha Truffle Filling on cake to within 1 inch of edges. Reroll cake. Chill till serving time. Sprinkle with cocoa powder and additional powdered sugar before serving. Makes 10 servings.

Mocha Truffle Filling: Dissolve 1 teaspoon *instant coffee crystals* in 2 tablespoons *hot water*. Beat ½ cup *margarine or butter* with an electric mixer on medium to high speed till softened. Mix ½ cup *unsweetened cocoa powder* and 1½ cups sifted *powdered sugar*. Alternately add cocoa powder mixture and 3 tablespoons *pasteurized egg product* to margarine, beating after each addition. Beat in coffee mixture, adding additional hot water, if necessary, to make of spreading consistency.

Nutrition facts per serving: 288 calories, 13 g total fat (2 g saturated fat), 85 mg cholesterol, 226 mg sodium, 39 g carbohydrate, 0 g fiber, 5 g protein.
Daily Value: 24% vitamin A, 0% vitamin C, 7% calcium, 9% iron.

CREME-FILLED FUDGE CAKES
The Chocolate Gloss doubles as a great ice cream topping.

2 cups all-purpose flour
⅓ cup unsweetened cocoa powder
1 teaspoon baking soda
⅛ teaspoon salt
½ cup shortening
1½ cups granulated sugar
2 eggs
1 cup water
   Vanilla Creme
   Chocolate Gloss
24 maraschino cherries (optional)

Line twenty-four 2½-inch muffin cups with paper bake cups. Combine flour, cocoa powder, baking soda, and salt. Set aside.

In a large mixing bowl beat shortening with an electric mixer on medium to high speed till softened. Add sugar; beat till combined. Add eggs, one at a time, beating well after each. Alternately add flour mixture and water, beating on low to medium speed after each addition just till combined. Pour into prepared muffin cups.

Bake in a 350° oven for 15 to 20 minutes or till a wooden toothpick inserted in centers comes out clean. Cool in pans on wire racks for 5 minutes. Remove from pans. Cool completely on wire racks.

Spoon Vanilla Creme into a pastry bag fitted with a large round tip or star tip. Push tip into tops of cupcakes and force some of the filling into each. Dip cupcake tops into Chocolate Gloss; let stand till set. Top with maraschino cherries, if desired. Makes 24 cupcakes.

Vanilla Creme: Beat 3 cups sifted *powdered sugar,* ½ cup *shortening,* ¼ cup *water,* and 1 teaspoon *vanilla* with electric mixer on low to medium speed till mixed. Beat 2 minutes on high speed or till fluffy.

Chocolate Gloss: In a medium saucepan combine 2 cups *miniature marshmallows,* ¾ cup *granulated sugar,* ½ cup *evaporated milk,* and ¼ cup *margarine or butter.* Cook and stir over medium heat till boiling. Boil 3 minutes, stirring constantly. Remove from heat; stir in 1 cup *semisweet chocolate pieces* till melted. Place bottom of saucepan in cold water. Beat by hand just till mixture begins to thicken.

Nutrition facts per serving: 313 calories, 14 g total fat (3 g saturated fat), 19 mg cholesterol, 99 mg sodium, 48 g carbohydrate, 0 g fiber, 3 g protein.
Daily Value: 3% vitamin A, 0% vitamin C, 2% calcium, 6% iron.

CHOCOLATE BOSTON CREAM PIE

Chocolate sponge cake, chocolate custard filling, and the traditional chocolate glaze make this version of Boston Cream Pie a chocolate lover's delight.

1   cup all-purpose flour
¼   cup unsweetened cocoa powder
4   egg yolks
⅓   cup water
1   teaspoon vanilla
⅔   cup granulated sugar
4   egg whites
¼   teaspoon cream of tartar
⅓   cup granulated sugar
     Chocolate Custard
     Chocolate Glaze
     Chocolate curls (optional)

Stir together flour and cocoa powder; set aside.

Beat egg yolks with electric mixer on high speed 5 minutes or till thick. Beat in water and vanilla on low speed. Gradually add ⅔ cup sugar beating on low to medium speed. Beat on medium to high speed till mixture thickens and doubles in volume (about 5 minutes total). Fold in flour mixture, sprinkling *¼ cup* over yolk mixture at a time. Wash beaters. Beat egg whites and cream of tartar till soft peaks form. Gradually add ⅓ cup sugar, beating till stiff peaks form. Fold *about 1 cup* of white mixture into yolk mixture; fold yolk mixture back into white mixture. Pour into ungreased 9-inch springform pan.

Bake in 325° oven 45 to 50 minutes or till top springs back when touched. Invert cake in pan. Cool. Remove from pan. Split cake into 2 layers. Fill with Chocolate Custard. Spread Chocolate Glaze over top. Chill till serving. If desired, top with chocolate curls. Serves 12.

Chocolate Custard: In heavy saucepan mix ⅔ cup *granulated sugar* and 2 tablespoons *cornstarch*. Stir in 1½ cups *milk* and 2 ounces *unsweetened chocolate,* chopped. Cook and stir till bubbly; cook and stir 2 minutes more. Remove from heat. Stir *1 cup* of hot mixture into 2 beaten *egg yolks*. Return to saucepan. Cook and stir 2 minutes more. Stir in 1 teaspoon *vanilla*. Cover with plastic wrap. Chill.

Chocolate Glaze: Melt 2 ounces *unsweetened chocolate* and 1 tablespoon *margarine or butter*. Remove from heat; stir in ¾ cup sifted *powdered sugar* and ½ teaspoon *vanilla*. Gradually add 4 to 8 teaspoons *hot water*, stirring till glaze is of a thin spreading consistency.

Nutrition facts per serving: 302 calories, 11 g total fat (4 g saturated fat), 180 mg cholesterol, 34 mg sodium, 48 g carbohydrate, 1 g fiber, 6 g protein.
Daily Value: 30% vitamin A, 0% vitamin C, 7% calcium, 12% iron.

SACHER TORTE

To decorate the cake as in the photo, add ¼ cup unsweetened cocoa powder to Sweetened Whipped Cream (page 22) and pipe on top of the cake.

⅔ cup margarine or butter
4 ounces unsweetened chocolate, chopped
6 egg yolks, slightly beaten
1 cup granulated sugar
6 egg whites
¼ cup granulated sugar
1 cup all-purpose flour
½ cup ground almonds
½ cup apricot preserves
   Semisweet Chocolate Glaze

Grease and lightly flour a 9-inch springform pan. In a saucepan heat and stir margarine or butter and unsweetened chocolate over low heat till melted; cool. Stir in egg yolks and 1 cup sugar. Set aside.

In a large mixing bowl beat egg whites with an electric mixer on medium to high speed till soft peaks form (tips curl). Gradually add ¼ cup sugar, about *2 tablespoons* at a time, beating till stiff peaks form (tips stand straight). Gently fold about *1 cup* of the egg white mixture into the egg yolk mixture. Then fold egg yolk mixture into remaining egg white mixture. Sprinkle flour and ground almonds over egg mixture; fold in gently, just till combined. Spread evenly in prepared pan.

Bake in a 325° oven for 40 to 50 minutes or till a wooden toothpick inserted in center comes out clean. Cool in pan on wire rack 10 minutes. Remove from pan. Cool completely on wire rack. Cut cake into 2 even layers. Place bottom layer, cut side up, on cake plate. Press apricot preserves through a sieve. Spread preserves over cake. Top with second layer. Pour Chocolate Glaze over top of cake, spreading evenly over top and sides of cake. Allow glaze to set completely, chilling, if necessary. Makes 12 servings.

Semisweet Chocolate Glaze: In a medium saucepan heat and stir ⅓ cup *light corn syrup,* 3 tablespoons *margarine or butter,* and 2 tablespoons *water* over medium heat till boiling. Remove from heat; stir in 1 6-ounce package (1 cup) *semisweet chocolate pieces* till melted. Cool to lukewarm, about 15 minutes. Stir till smooth.

Nutrition facts per serving: 474 calories, 27 g total fat (5 g saturated fat), 107 mg cholesterol, 193 mg sodium, 58 g carbohydrate, 1 g fiber, 7 g protein.
Daily Value: 32% vitamin A, 0% vitamin C, 4% calcium, 16% iron.

VIENNESE CHOCOLATE TORTE

This ultra-sumptuous dessert is at its best if you let it stand at room temperature for 30 minutes before serving. Then top it with white chocolate curls and serve.

White Chocolate Ganache
3 ounces unsweetened chocolate
1 cup water
2¼ cups all-purpose flour
1½ teaspoons baking soda
½ teaspoon salt
½ cup margarine or butter
2 cups granulated sugar
1 teaspoon vanilla
3 eggs
1 cup buttermilk or sour milk (see note, page 18)
    Chocolate Mousse

Grease and flour two 9x1½-inch round baking pans. Heat chocolate and water till chocolate melts; cool. Mix flour, soda, and salt.

In large mixing bowl beat margarine with an electric mixer on medium to high speed till softened. Add sugar and vanilla; beat till mixed. Add eggs, one at a time, beating well after each. Combine chocolate mixture and buttermilk. Alternately add flour mixture and chocolate mixture, beating on low to medium speed after each addition just till combined. Pour batter into prepared pans. Bake in 350° oven 30 to 35 minutes or till a toothpick inserted in centers comes out clean. Cool in pans on wire racks 10 minutes. Remove from pans. Cool completely on wire racks. Split cake layers in half. Spread *¾ cup* of the Chocolate Mousse on each layer; stack layers. Frost sides of cake with White Chocolate Ganache. Store in refrigerator. Let stand 30 minutes at room temperature before serving. Serves 16.

White Chocolate Ganache: Heat 1 cup *whipping cream* till simmering. Remove from heat; add one 6-ounce package *white baking bar, chopped,* stirring till melted. Stir in 1 teaspoon *vanilla.* Cover with plastic wrap. Chill for 3 to 6 hours. To frost cake, beat with electric mixer on medium speed just till soft peaks form. *Do not* overbeat.

Chocolate Mousse: In saucepan melt 2 cups *semisweet chocolate pieces.* Beat together ¼ cup *water* and 4 *egg yolks.* Gradually stir *half* of chocolate into yolk mixture. Return to saucepan. Cook and stir over medium heat till bubbly and slightly thickened. Remove from heat. Stir in ½ teaspoon ground *cinnamon* and ½ teaspoon *vanilla.* Cool. Fold chocolate mixture into 1 cup *whipping cream, whipped.*

Nutrition facts per serving: 529 calories, 31 g total fat (12 g saturated fat), 135 mg cholesterol, 304 mg sodium, 62 g carbohydrate, 1 g fiber, 7 g protein.
Daily Value: 30% vitamin A, 0% vitamin C, 7% calcium, 13% iron.

LEMON ROLL-UP

A tantalizingly tart lemon filling fills this deliciously tender sponge cake roll with a wealth of flavor.

½ cup all-purpose flour
1 teaspoon baking powder
¼ teaspoon salt
4 egg yolks
½ teaspoon vanilla
⅓ cup granulated sugar
2 teaspoons finely shredded lemon peel
4 egg whites
½ cup granulated sugar
   Sifted powdered sugar
   Lemon Filling
   Lemon twists (optional)
   Lemon leaves (optional)

Grease and flour a 15x10x1-inch jelly-roll pan. Stir together flour, baking powder, and salt. Set aside.

In a small mixing bowl beat egg yolks and vanilla with an electric mixer on high speed about 5 minutes or till thick and lemon-colored. Gradually add ⅓ cup sugar, beating on medium speed till sugar is almost dissolved. Stir in lemon peel. Thoroughly wash beaters.

In large bowl beat egg whites on medium to high speed till soft peaks form (tips curl). Gradually add ½ cup sugar, beating till stiff peaks form (tips stand straight). Fold yolk mixture into whites. Fold flour mixture into egg mixture just till combined. Spread in prepared pan.

Bake in 375° oven for 12 to 15 minutes or till top springs back when lightly touched. Immediately loosen edges of cake from pan; turn out onto a towel sprinkled with sifted powdered sugar. Starting with a narrow end, roll up cake and towel together. Cool on wire rack.

Unroll cake. Spread Lemon Filling on cake to within 1 inch of edges. Reroll cake without towel. Chill at least 2 hours or till ready to serve. Garnish with lemon twists and leaves, if desired. Makes 10 servings.

Lemon Filling: In a medium saucepan combine ½ cup *granulated sugar* and 4 teaspoons *cornstarch*. Stir in ½ cup *cold water* and 2 beaten *egg yolks*. Cook and stir over medium heat till bubbly; cook and stir 2 minutes more. Remove from heat; stir in 1 tablespoon *margarine or butter*, 2 teaspoons finely shredded *lemon peel*, and 2 tablespoons *lemon juice*. Cover surface with plastic wrap. Chill well.

Nutrition facts per serving: 185 calories, 4 g total fat (1 g saturated fat), 128 mg cholesterol, 130 mg sodium, 34 g carbohydrate, 0 g fiber, 4 g protein.
Daily Value: 20% vitamin A, 4% vitamin C, 4% calcium, 4% iron.

PUMPKIN CAKE ROLL

A cinnamon- and ginger-spiced cake encircles a cream cheese filling, studded with pecans and currants—
a perfect flavor combination for an autumn dessert.

¾ cup all-purpose flour
2 teaspoons ground cinnamon
1 teaspoon baking powder
1 teaspoon ground ginger
¼ teaspoon salt
3 eggs
1 cup granulated sugar
⅔ cup canned pumpkin
  Sifted powdered sugar
  Fruit and Nut Filling
  Kumquat flowers (optional)

Grease and flour a 15x10x1-inch jelly-roll pan. Stir together flour, cinnamon, baking powder, ginger, and salt. Set aside.

In a large mixing bowl beat eggs with an electric mixer on high speed about 5 minutes or till thick and lemon-colored. Gradually add sugar, beating on medium speed till sugar is almost dissolved. Stir in pumpkin. Sprinkle flour mixture over egg mixture; fold in gently, just till combined. Spread batter evenly into prepared pan.

Bake in a 350° oven about 15 minutes or till top springs back when lightly touched. Immediately loosen edges of cake from pan; turn out onto a towel sprinkled with powdered sugar. Starting with a narrow end, roll up warm cake and towel together. Cool on a wire rack.

Unroll cake. Spread Fruit and Nut Filling on cake to within 1 inch of edges. Reroll cake without towel. Chill at least 2 hours or till ready to serve. Garnish with kumquat flowers, if desired. Makes 10 servings.

Fruit and Nut Filling: In a chilled medium mixing bowl, combine two 3-ounce packages *cream cheese*, ¼ cup *margarine or butter*, and ½ teaspoon *vanilla*. Beat with an electric mixer on medium to high speed till smooth. Beat in 1 cup sifted *powdered sugar* till smooth. Stir in ½ cup chopped *pecans* and ⅓ cup dried *currants or snipped raisins*.

Nutrition facts per serving: 331 calories, 16 g total fat (5 g saturated fat), 83 mg cholesterol, 215 mg sodium, 45 g carbohydrate, 1 g fiber, 5 g protein.
Daily Value: 51% vitamin A, 1% vitamin C, 11% calcium, 11% iron.

RICOTTA CAKE ROLL-UP

Almond brickle chips flavor the creamy ricotta filling and adorn the satiny chocolate glaze.

½	cup all-purpose flour
1	teaspoon baking powder
¼	teaspoon salt
4	egg yolks
½	teaspoon vanilla
⅓	cup granulated sugar
4	egg whites
¼	teaspoon cream of tartar
½	cup granulated sugar
	Sifted powdered sugar
	Ricotta Filling
	Chocolate Icing
2	tablespoons almond brickle chips

Grease and lightly flour a 15x10x1-inch jelly-roll pan. Stir together flour, baking powder, and salt. Set aside.

Beat egg yolks and vanilla with an electric mixer on high speed about 5 minutes or till thick and lemon-colored. Gradually add ⅓ cup sugar, beating on medium speed till sugar is almost dissolved. Wash beaters.

In a large mixing bowl beat egg whites and cream of tartar on medium to high speed till soft peaks form (tips curl). Gradually add ½ cup sugar, beating till stiff peaks form (tips stand straight). Fold yolk mixture into whites. Sprinkle the flour mixture over egg mixture; fold in gently, just till combined. Spread evenly in prepared pan.

Bake in 375° oven for 12 to 15 minutes or till top springs back when lightly touched. Immediately loosen edges of cake; turn out onto towel sprinkled with powdered sugar. Starting with a narrow end, roll up cake and towel together. Cool on wire rack. Unroll cake. Spread Ricotta Filling on cake to within 1 inch of edges. Reroll cake. Frost with Chocolate Icing. Chill 2 hours or till serving time. Sprinkle with the almond brickle chips just before serving. Makes 10 servings.

Ricotta Filling: Stir together 1 cup *ricotta cheese*, ¼ cup *granulated sugar*, ½ teaspoon *vanilla*, and a few drops *almond extract*. Stir in ⅓ cup *almond brickle chips*.

Chocolate Icing: Beat 1 cup sifted *powdered sugar*, 2 tablespoons *unsweetened cocoa powder*, 1 tablespoon *light corn syrup*, ¼ teaspoon *vanilla*, and enough *milk* (1 tablespoon) till spreading consistency.

Nutrition facts per serving: 263 calories, 7 g total fat (2 g saturated fat), 95 mg cholesterol, 179 mg sodium, 45 g carbohydrate, 0 g fiber, 6 g protein.
Daily Value: 16% vitamin A, 0% vitamin C, 10% calcium, 6% iron.

APRICOT-HAZELNUT CAKE ROLL

Once you spread the batter in the pan, sprinkle it with nuts to create this stunning nut-covered dessert roll.

1 cup all-purpose flour
1 teaspoon baking powder
¼ teaspoon salt
½ teaspoon apple pie spice
1 8¾-ounce can unpeeled apricot halves
   (in syrup)
2 tablespoons granulated sugar
3 eggs
½ cup granulated sugar
¾ cup finely chopped hazelnuts or
   pecans
   Sifted powdered sugar
   Cream Cheese Filling

Grease and lightly flour a 15x10x1-inch jelly-roll pan. Stir together flour, baking powder, salt, and apple pie spice. Set aside.

Drain apricots, reserving ⅓ cup syrup. Finely chop apricots. In a small saucepan combine chopped apricots, reserved apricot syrup, and 2 tablespoons sugar. Bring apricot mixture to boiling; reduce heat to low. Cook, stirring and mashing with a spoon, about 4 minutes or till thickened. Remove from heat; cool to room temperature. Set aside.

In a large mixing bowl beat eggs with an electric mixer on high speed about 5 minutes or till thick and lemon-colored. Gradually add apricot mixture and ½ cup sugar, beating on medium speed till sugar is almost dissolved. Sprinkle flour mixture over egg mixture; fold in gently, just till combined. Spread batter evenly in prepared pan. Sprinkle with nuts.

Bake in a 375° oven for 12 to 15 minutes or till top springs back when lightly touched. Immediately loosen edges of cake; turn out onto a towel sprinkled with powdered sugar. Starting with a narrow end, roll up warm cake and towel together. Cool on a wire rack. Unroll cake. Spread Cream Cheese Filling on cake to within 1 inch of edges. Reroll cake without towel. Chill for 2 to 24 hours. Serves 10.

Cream Cheese Filling: In a small mixing bowl combine two 3-ounce packages *cream cheese*, softened; ¼ cup *margarine or butter*, softened; and ½ teaspoon *vanilla*. Beat with an electric mixer on medium to high speed till fluffy. Beat in 1½ cups sifted *powdered sugar* and 1 tablespoon *milk*.

Nutrition facts per serving: 351 calories, 18 g total fat (6 g saturated fat), 83 mg cholesterol, 217 mg sodium, 45 g carbohydrate, 2 g fiber, 6 g protein.
Daily Value: 19% vitamin A, 1% vitamin C, 6% calcium, 9% iron.

WHOLE WHEAT CAKE ROLL

Wheat germ gives a nutty flavor and just a bit of crunch to the cake. It pairs up deliciously with the mixed dried fruit filling.

⅓ to ½ cup toasted wheat germ
¼ cup all-purpose flour
¼ cup whole wheat flour
1 teaspoon baking powder
¼ teaspoon salt
4 egg yolks
½ teaspoon vanilla
⅓ cup granulated sugar
4 egg whites
½ cup granulated sugar
   Sifted powdered sugar
   Fruit Filling
   Sweetened Whipped Cream
     (see recipe, page 22) (optional)

Grease a 15x10x1-inch jelly-roll pan; sprinkle with wheat germ. Stir together all-purpose flour, whole wheat flour, baking powder, and salt. Set aside.

In a medium mixing bowl beat egg yolks and vanilla with an electric mixer on high speed about 5 minutes or till thick and lemon-colored. Gradually add ⅓ cup sugar, beating on medium speed till sugar is almost dissolved. Thoroughly wash beaters.

In a large mixing bowl beat egg whites on medium to high speed till soft peaks form (tips curl). Gradually add ½ cup sugar, beating till stiff peaks form (tips stand straight). Fold egg yolk mixture into egg white mixture. Sprinkle flour mixture over egg mixture; fold in gently, just till combined. Spread batter evenly in prepared pan.

Bake in 375° oven 12 to 15 minutes or till top springs back when touched. Loosen edges of cake from pan; turn out onto a towel sprinkled with powdered sugar. Starting with a narrow end, roll up warm cake and towel together. Cool on a wire rack. Unroll cake. Spread Fruit Filling on cake to within 1 inch of edges. Reroll cake without towel. Serve with Sweetened Whipped Cream, if desired. Serves 10.

Fruit Filling: In a medium saucepan mix ¾ cup *diced mixed dried fruits* and 1½ cups *apple juice.* Bring to boiling; reduce heat. Cover and simmer for 10 minutes. Stir together 2 tablespoons *cornstarch* and 1 tablespoon *granulated sugar*; stir into fruit mixture. Cook and stir till thickened and bubbly. Cook and stir 2 minutes more.

Nutrition facts per serving: 185 calories, 3 g total fat (1 g saturated fat), 85 mg cholesterol, 69 mg sodium, 37 g carbohydrate, 1 g fiber, 5 g protein.
Daily Value: 14% vitamin A, 1% vitamin C, 4% calcium, 7% iron.

DAFFODIL CAKE

Celebrate the rites of spring with this classic angel food cake marbled with lemon-yellow sponge cake. It's only fitting to create a simple centerpiece with daffodils from your garden.

1½ cups egg whites (11 or 12 large)
1   cup sifted cake flour or sifted all-
      purpose flour
¾   cup granulated sugar
2   teaspoons vanilla
1½ teaspoons cream of tartar
¼   teaspoon salt
¾   cup sugar
6   egg yolks
1½ teaspoons finely shredded lemon peel
      Tangy Lemon Frosting
      Finely shredded lemon peel (optional)

In a very large mixing bowl allow egg whites to stand at room temperature for 30 minutes. Meanwhile, sift together cake flour or all-purpose flour and ¾ cup sugar 3 times; set aside.

Add vanilla, cream of tartar, and salt to egg whites. Beat with electric mixer on medium to high speed till soft peaks form (tips curl). Gradually add ¾ cup sugar, *2 tablespoons* at a time, beating till stiff peaks form (tips stand straight). Sift *one-fourth* of the flour mixture over white mixture; fold in gently. (If bowl is too full, transfer to larger bowl.) Repeat with remaining flour mixture, using *one-fourth* of the flour mixture each time. Transfer *half* of the batter to another bowl.

In a small mixing bowl beat egg yolks on high speed 6 minutes or till thick and lemon-colored. Fold in 1½ teaspoons lemon peel. Gently fold yolk mixture into *half* of the egg white mixture. Alternately spoon yellow batter and remaining white batter into an ungreased 10-inch tube pan. Swirl metal spatula through batters to marble.

Bake on the lowest rack in a 350° oven for 40 to 45 minutes or till top springs back when lightly touched. Immediately invert cake in pan; cool completely. Loosen sides of cake from pan; remove. Place cake upside down on plate; frost with Tangy Lemon Frosting. Sprinkle top with finely shredded lemon peel, if desired. Serves 12.

Tangy Lemon Frosting: Beat ½ cup *margarine or butter* with an electric mixer till softened. Beat in 5½ cups sifted *powdered sugar*, ½ teaspoon finely shredded *lemon peel*, and ⅓ cup *lemon juice*, adding additional lemon juice, if necessary, to make of spreading consistency.

Nutrition facts per serving: 424 calories, 10 g total fat (2 g saturated fat), 107 mg cholesterol, 189 mg sodium, 79 g carbohydrate, 0 g fiber, 5 g protein.
Daily Value: 25% vitamin A, 5% vitamin C, 1% calcium, 6% iron.

NUTMEG-COCONUT CHIFFON CAKE

Chiffon cakes are a cross between cakes made with shortening and the light and airy angel food and sponge cakes. This handsome beauty is baked in a tube pan and split so it can be filled and frosted with whipped cream, and tropically flavored with cream of coconut.

2¼ cups sifted cake flour or 2 cups all-purpose flour
1½ cups granulated sugar
1 tablespoon baking powder
1 teaspoon ground nutmeg
⅛ teaspoon salt
7 egg yolks
½ cup cold water
⅓ cup cooking oil
⅓ cup cream of coconut
7 egg whites
½ teaspoon cream of tartar
Coconut Whipped Cream
1 cup flaked coconut, toasted

In a large mixing bowl mix flour, sugar, baking powder, nutmeg, and salt. Make a well in the center of the flour mixture. Add egg yolks, water, oil, and cream of coconut. Beat with an electric mixer on low to medium speed till combined. Beat on high speed about 5 minutes or till smooth. Transfer to another bowl. Thoroughly wash beaters.

In a very large mixing bowl beat egg whites and cream of tartar on medium to high speed till stiff peaks form (tips stand straight). Pour batter in a thin stream over egg white mixture, folding in gently just till combined. Pour batter into an ungreased 10-inch tube pan.

Bake in a 325° oven for 65 to 70 minutes or till top springs back when lightly touched. Immediately invert cake in pan; cool completely. Loosen sides of cake from pan; remove. Split cake in half horizontally with a thin, long-bladed knife.

Place bottom layer on cake plate. Spread about ¾ *cup* of the Coconut Whipped Cream over layer. Sprinkle with *half* of the coconut. Top with remaining cake layer. Frost with remaining Coconut Whipped Cream. Sprinkle with remaining coconut. Store in the refrigerator. Makes 12 servings.

Coconut Whipped Cream: In a chilled medium mixing bowl combine 2 cups *whipping cream* and ¼ cup *cream of coconut*. Beat with an electric mixer on medium to high speed till soft peaks form.

Nutrition information per serving: 441 calories, 29 g total fat (11 g saturated fat), 153 mg cholesterol, 173 mg sodium, 41 g carbohydrate, 0 g fiber, 6 g protein.
Daily Value: *31% vitamin A, 0% vitamin C, 9% calcium, 11% iron.*

STRAWBERRY-CREAM SPONGE CAKE

Cut a slice of this sponge cake and you're in for a treat—the hollowed-out center is stuffed with fresh strawberries and whipped cream!

1¼ cups all-purpose flour
⅓ cup granulated sugar
6 egg yolks
½ cup cold water
1½ teaspoons vanilla
⅔ cup granulated sugar
6 egg whites
1 teaspoon cream of tartar
¼ teaspoon salt
½ cup granulated sugar
  Strawberry Cream
  Fresh strawberries (optional)
  Sweetened Whipped Cream (see recipe, page 22)

Combine flour and the ⅓ cup sugar. Set aside.

Beat egg yolks with electric mixer on high speed 6 minutes or till thick and lemon-colored. Add water and vanilla. Beat on low speed till mixed. Gradually add ⅔ cup sugar, beating on medium speed 5 minutes or till sugar is almost dissolved. Gradually add *one-fourth* of flour mixture, beating on low speed just till moistened. Repeat with remaining flour mixture, using *one-fourth* each time. Wash beaters.

Beat egg whites, cream of tartar, and salt on medium to high speed till soft peaks form. Add ½ cup sugar, *2 tablespoons* at a time, beating till stiff peaks form. Stir *1 cup* of the white mixture into yolk mixture. Fold yolk mixture back into remaining white mixture. Pour into ungreased 10-inch tube pan. Cut through batter with metal spatula.

Bake in a 325° oven 60 to 65 minutes or till top springs back when lightly touched. Immediately invert cake in pan; cool well. Loosen sides of cake; remove. Cut off top 1 inch of the cake; set aside. Cut around hole in center, leaving a 1-inch thickness around hole. Then cut around the outer edge of the cake, leaving outer cake wall 1 inch thick. Using a spoon, remove center of cake, leaving a 1-inch-thick base. Spoon Strawberry Cream into the hollowed-out section. Replace the top of the cake. Chill for 4 to 24 hours. Serve with fresh strawberries and Sweeteend Whipped Cream, if desired. Serves 12.

Strawberry Cream: Combine 2 cups coarsely chopped *strawberries* and ⅓ cup *granulated sugar;* let stand 30 minutes. Beat 1 cup *whipping cream* till soft peaks form. Fold strawberry mixture into cream.

Nutrition information per serving: 278 calories, 10 g total fat (5 g saturated fat), 134 mg cholesterol, 84 mg sodium, 43 g carbohydrate, 1 g fiber, 5 g protein.
Daily Value: 24% vitamin A, 23% vitamin C, 2% calcium, 6% iron.

MILE-HIGH ANGEL FOOD CAKE

As with any angel, chiffon, or sponge cake, it is especially important that the egg whites be warmed to room temperature. At room temperature the whites can incorporate more air during beating—the more air you beat in, the higher the cake!

1½   cups egg whites (11 or 12 large)
1½   cups sifted powdered sugar
 1   cup sifted cake flour or sifted all-
        purpose flour
1½   teaspoons cream of tartar
 1   teaspoon vanilla
 ¼   teaspoon salt
 1   cup granulated sugar
     Sliced strawberries and/or kiwi fruit
        (optional)

In a very large mixing bowl allow egg whites to stand at room temperature for 30 minutes. Meanwhile, sift together powdered sugar and flour 3 times. Set aside.

Add cream of tartar, vanilla, and salt to egg whites. Beat with an electric mixer on medium to high speed till soft peaks form (tips curl). Gradually add granulated sugar, about *2 tablespoons* at a time, beating till stiff peaks form (tips stand straight).

Sift about *one-fourth* of the flour mixture over the egg white mixture; fold in gently. (If bowl is too full, transfer to larger bowl.) Repeat with remaining flour mixture, using about *one-fourth* of the flour mixture each time. Spoon batter into an ungreased 10-inch tube pan. Gently cut through batter with a knife or metal spatula to remove any large air pockets.

Bake on the lowest rack in a 350° oven about 40 minutes or till top springs back when lightly touched. Immediately invert cake in pan; cool completely. Loosen sides of cake from pan; remove. Serve with sliced strawberries and/or kiwi fruit, if desired. Makes 12 servings.

Nutrition information per serving: 163 calories, 0 g total fat (0 g saturated fat), 0 mg cholesterol, 95 mg sodium, 37 g carbohydrate, 0 g fiber, 4 g protein.
Daily Value: 0% vitamin A, 0% vitamin C, 0% calcium, 4% iron.

HONEY ANGEL CAKE

A taste of honey, used in place of some of the sugar, gives this cake its distinctively sweet flavor.

1½ cups egg whites (11 to 12 large)
1½ cups sifted powdered sugar
1   cup sifted cake flour or sifted all-
    purpose flour
1½ teaspoons cream of tartar
1   teaspoon vanilla
¼   cup honey
½   cup granulated sugar
    Sliced fresh strawberries (optional)

In a very large mixing bowl allow egg whites to stand at room temperature for 30 minutes. Meanwhile, sift together powdered sugar and flour 3 times; set aside.

Add cream of tartar and vanilla to egg whites. Beat with an electric mixer on medium to high speed till soft peaks form (tips curl). Gradually pour honey in a thin stream over the egg white mixture. Gradually add the sugar, about *2 tablespoons* at a time, beating till stiff peaks form (tips stand straight).

Sift about *one-fourth* of the flour mixture over the egg white mixture; fold in gently. (If bowl is too full, transfer to a larger bowl.) Repeat with remaining flour mixture, using about *one-fourth* of the flour mixture each time. Spoon batter into an ungreased 10-inch tube pan. Gently cut through batter with a knife or narrow metal spatula to remove any large air pockets.

Bake on the lowest rack in a 350° oven for 40 to 45 minutes or till top springs back when lightly touched. Immediately invert cake in pan; cool completely. Loosen sides of cake from pan; remove. Serve with sliced strawberries, if desired. Makes 12 servings.

Nutrition information per serving: 152 calories, 0 g total fat (0 g saturated fat), 0 mg cholesterol, 51 mg sodium, 34 g carbohydrate, 0 g fiber, 4 g protein.
Daily Value: 0% vitamin A, 0% vitamin C, 0% calcium, 4% iron.

PINEAPPLE-GINGER CHIFFON CAKE

Crowned with pineapple chunks, this tall and handsome cake makes an impressive show for showers, graduations, birthdays, and any other celebrations.

2   cups all-purpose flour
1½ cups granulated sugar
1   tablespoon baking powder
1   teaspoon ground ginger
½   teaspoon salt
¼   teaspoon baking soda
¾   cup pineapple juice
½   cup cooking oil
7   egg yolks
7   egg whites
½   teaspoon cream of tartar
      Vanilla Whipped Cream
      Canned pineapple chunks,
         well drained (optional)

In a large mixing bowl stir together flour, sugar, baking powder, ginger, salt, and baking soda. Make a well in the center of the flour mixture. Add pineapple juice, oil, and egg yolks. Beat with an electric mixer on low to medium speed about 1 minute or till smooth. Transfer to another bowl. Thoroughly wash beaters.

In a very large mixing bowl beat egg whites and cream of tartar on medium to high speed till stiff peaks form (tips stand straight). Pour batter in a thin stream over egg white mixture, folding in gently just till combined. Pour batter into an ungreased 10-inch tube pan.

Bake in a 325° oven for 65 to 70 minutes or till top springs back when lightly touched. Immediately invert cake in pan; cool completely. Loosen sides of cake from pan; remove cake. Place cake upside down on plate. Frost with Vanilla Whipped Cream. Store cake, covered, in the refrigerator. Top with pineapple chunks just before serving, if desired. Makes 12 servings.

Vanilla Whipped Cream: In a chilled medium mixing bowl combine 2 cups *whipping cream,* ¼ cup *granulated sugar,* and 1 teaspoon *vanilla.* Beat with an electric mixer on medium to high speed till soft peaks form.

Nutrition information per serving: 455 calories, 27 g total fat (11 g saturated fat), 179 mg cholesterol, 258 mg sodium, 48 g carbohydrate, 1 g fiber, 7 g protein.
Daily Value: 36% vitamin A, 3% vitamin C, 10% calcium, 9% iron.

HOT MILK SPONGE CAKE WITH FLUFFY PINK FROSTING

Crowned with fluffy pink frosting, this easy-to-make sponge cake is perfect for birthday parties for little girls.

2 cups all-purpose flour
2 teaspoons baking powder
½ teaspoon salt
4 eggs
2 cups granulated sugar
1 cup milk
¼ cup margarine or butter
Fluffy Pink Frosting

Grease a 13x9x2-inch baking pan and line with waxed paper; grease waxed paper. Combine flour, baking powder, and salt. Set aside.

In a large mixing bowl beat eggs with an electric mixer on high speed about 4 minutes or till thick and lemon-colored. Gradually add sugar, about *2 tablespoons* at a time, beating on medium speed about 5 minutes or till sugar is almost dissolved. Add flour mixture to egg mixture, stirring just till combined.

In small sauce pan heat milk with margarine or butter till margarine or butter melts; stir into batter till combined. Pour batter into the prepared pan.

Bake in a 350° oven for 25 to 30 minutes or till top springs back when lightly touched. Cool in pan on wire rack 10 minutes. Remove from pan; remove waxed paper. Cool completely on a wire rack. Frost top and sides with Fluffy Pink Frosting. Makes 15 servings.

Fluffy Pink Frosting: In top of a double boiler combine 1½ cups *granulated sugar*, ⅓ cup *cold water*, 2 *egg whites*, 2 teaspoons *light corn syrup* or ¼ teaspoon *cream of tartar*, and dash *salt*. Beat 30 seconds with an electric mixer on low to medium speed. Place over boiling water (upper pan should not touch water). Cook about 9 minutes while beating constantly on medium to high speed or till stiff glossy peaks form. Remove from heat; add 1 teaspoon *vanilla* and 3 drops *red food coloring*. Beat 2 to 3 minutes more or till frosting is of spreading consistency. Use immediately.

Nutrition information per serving: 298 calories, 5 g total fat (1 g saturated fat), 58 mg cholesterol, 198 mg sodium, 60 g carbohydrate, 0 g fiber, 4 g protein.
Daily Value: 7% vitamin A, 0% vitamin C, 6% calcium, 6% iron.

BANANA CHIFFON CAKE

Enhance the fresh banana flavor of this velvety cake by topping it with a mixture of your favorite fresh fruits. And then, pile on lots of whipped cream.

2¼ cups sifted cake flour or 2 cups all-
       purpose flour
1½ cups granulated sugar
 1   tablespoon baking powder
 ½   teaspoon salt
 1   cup mashed ripe bananas (3 medium)
 ½   cup cooking oil
 5   egg yolks
 ¼   cup cold water
 1   teaspoon finely shredded lemon peel
 8   egg whites
 1   teaspoon cream of tartar
 2   cups sliced fresh strawberries, kiwi
       fruit, and/or bananas
       Sweetened Whipped Cream
       (see recipe, page 22) (optional)

In a large mixing bowl stir together flour, sugar, baking powder, and salt. Make a well in the center of the flour mixture. Add mashed bananas, oil, egg yolks, and water. Beat with an electric mixer on low to medium speed till combined. Beat on high speed 1 minute or till smooth. Fold in lemon peel. Thoroughly wash beaters.

In a very large mixing bowl beat egg whites and cream of tartar on medium to high speed till stiff peaks form (tips stand straight). Fold about *1 cup* of the beaten egg white mixture into banana batter to lighten. Pour banana batter in a thin stream over remaining egg white mixture, folding in gently just till combined. Pour batter into an ungreased 10-inch tube pan.

Bake in a 325° oven for 60 to 65 minutes or till top springs back when lightly touched. Immediately invert cake in pan; cool completely. Loosen sides of cake from pan; remove. Serve with fresh fruit, and, if desired, Sweetened Whipped Cream. Makes 12 servings.

Nutrition information per serving: 321 calories, 12 g total fat (2 g saturated fat), 89 mg cholesterol, 221 mg sodium, 50 g carbohydrate, 1 g fiber, 6 g protein.
Daily Value: 13% vitamin A, 28% vitamin C, 8% calcium, 12% iron.

ORANGE SUNSHINE CAKE

After icing the cake use a cake comb (available where kitchen supplies and cake decorating equipment are sold) to give the frosting this fancy professional look. For a finishing touch, add a border of whipped cream and a sprinkling of orange peel.

2 cups all-purpose flour
1½ cups granulated sugar
1 tablespoon baking powder
½ teaspoon salt
½ cup cooking oil
5 egg yolks
2 teaspoons finely shredded orange peel (set aside)
½ cup orange juice
¼ cup cold water
1 cup egg whites (7 or 8 large)
1 teaspoon cream of tartar
Creamy Orange Frosting
Sweetened Whipped Cream (see recipe, page 22) (optional)
Thin orange peel curls (optional)

Grease bottoms of three 9x1½-inch round baking pans. Line with waxed paper. Set aside.

In a bowl combine flour, sugar, baking powder, and salt. Make a well in the center of the flour mixture. Add oil, egg yolks, orange juice, and water. Beat with an electric mixer on low to medium speed about 1 minute or till smooth. Fold in orange peel. Wash beaters.

In a very large mixing bowl beat egg whites and cream of tartar on medium to high speed till stiff peaks form (tips stand straight). Pour batter in a thin stream over egg white mixture, folding in gently just till combined. Pour batter into prepared pans.

Bake in a 350° oven for 25 to 30 minutes or till tops spring back when lightly touched. Immediately invert cakes in pans onto wire racks; cool completely. Loosen sides of cakes from pans. Remove cakes; remove waxed paper. Spread ½ *cup* of the Creamy Orange Frosting on each of *two* of the layers. Stack layers; top with remaining layer. Frost sides and top of cake with remaining Creamy Orange Frosting. If desired, pipe a decorative border with Sweetened Whipped Cream and top with orange peel curls. Makes 12 servings.

Creamy Orange Frosting: Beat 1¼ cups *shortening*, 1½ teaspoons *vanilla,* and 1 teaspoon *orange extract* with an electric mixer on medium to high speed for 30 seconds. Gradually beat in 3 cups sifted *powdered sugar.* Add 4 tablespoons *milk* and, if desired, several drops of *red and yellow food coloring.* Beat in enough additional sifted *powdered sugar* (about 2⅓ cups) to make of spreading consistency.

Nutrition information per serving: 652 calories, 33 g total fat (7g saturated fat), 89 mg cholesterol, 218 mg sodium, 86 g carbohydrate, 1 g fiber, 5 g protein.
Daily Value: 13% vitamin A, 9% vitamin C, 8% calcium, 9% iron.

POUND CAKE

Pound cake, so aptly named, originally was made with a pound each of butter, sugar, eggs, and flour. We cut the recipe, but kept the rich flavor.

1   **cup butter (no substitutes)**
4   **eggs**
2   **cups all-purpose flour**
1   **teaspoon baking powder**
¼   **teaspoon ground nutmeg (optional)**
1   **cup granulated sugar**
1   **teaspoon vanilla**
    Sifted powdered sugar (optional)

Bring butter and eggs to room temperature. Meanwhile, grease and lightly flour a 9x5x3-inch loaf pan. Combine flour, baking powder, and, if desired, nutmeg. Set aside.

In a large mixing bowl beat butter with an electric mixer on medium to high speed for 30 seconds or till softened. Gradually add sugar, *2 tablespoons* at a time, beating on medium speed about 6 minutes or till very light and fluffy. Add vanilla. Add eggs, one at a time, beating on low to medium speed 1 minute after each addition and scraping bowl frequently. Gradually add flour mixture, beating on low speed just till combined. Pour batter into prepared pan.

Bake in a 325° oven for 55 to 65 minutes or till a wooden toothpick inserted in center comes out clean. Cool in pan on a wire rack for 10 minutes. Remove from pan. Cool completely on wire rack. Sprinkle with powdered sugar, if desired. Makes 10 to 12 servings.

Nutrition information per serving: 353 calories, 20 g total fat (12 g saturated fat), 134 mg cholesterol, 248 mg sodium, 38 g carbohydrate, 1 g fiber, 5 g protein.
Daily Value: 20% vitamin A, 0% vitamin C, 4% calcium, 9% iron.

PUMPKIN RAISIN POUND CAKE

This brown sugar pound cake is filled with the rich flavors of autumn—pumpkin, brown sugar, and spices.

1 cup butter (no substitutes)
3 eggs
3 cups all-purpose flour
4 teaspoons baking powder
1½ teaspoons ground cinnamon
½ teaspoon ground nutmeg
¼ teaspoon baking soda
¼ teaspoon salt
¼ teaspoon ground cloves
1 cup granulated sugar
1 cup packed brown sugar
1 teaspoon vanilla
1⅓ cups canned pumpkin
½ cup milk
¾ cup raisins
Pumpkin Glaze

Bring butter and eggs to room temperature. Meanwhile, grease and lightly flour a 10-inch fluted tube pan. Combine flour, baking powder, cinnamon, nutmeg, baking soda, salt, and cloves. Set aside.

In a large mixing bowl beat butter with an electric mixer on medium to high speed about 30 seconds or till softened. Gradually add granulated sugar and brown sugar, *2 tablespoons* at a time, beating on medium speed about 6 minutes or till very light and fluffy. Add vanilla. Add eggs, one at a time, beating on low to medium speed for 1 minute after each addition and scraping bowl frequently. Gradually add flour mixture, pumpkin, and milk alternately to beaten mixture, beating on low speed just till combined. Stir in raisins. Pour batter into prepared pan.

Bake in a 325° oven about 1¼ hours or till a wooden toothpick inserted in center comes out clean. Cool in pan on wire rack 15 minutes. Remove from pan. Cool completely on wire rack. Drizzle with Pumpkin Glaze. Makes 16 to 20 servings.

Pumpkin Glaze: In a small mixing bowl stir together 1 cup sifted *powdered sugar*, 1 tablespoon *canned pumpkin*, ¼ teaspoon *vanilla*, and 2 to 3 teaspoons *milk* to make a thick glaze.

Nutrition information per serving: 351 calories, 13 g total fat (8 g saturated fat), 71 mg cholesterol, 284 mg sodium, 57 g carbohydrate, 1 g fiber, 4 g protein.
Daily Value: 59% vitamin A, 2% vitamin C, 10% calcium, 13% iron.

FRUIT-NUT LOAF

Time for a coffee break? Slip a slice of this orange-scented cake into the toaster for a mid-morning or afternoon snack.

1   **cup butter (no substitutes)**
4   **eggs**
2   **cups all-purpose flour**
1   **teaspoon baking powder**
¼   **teaspoon salt**
1   **cup granulated sugar**
1   **tablespoon finely shredded orange peel**
1   **teaspoon vanilla**
½   **cup finely chopped pecans**
½   **cup currants, raisins, and/or snipped dried cherries**
    Orange Icing

Bring butter and eggs to room temperature. Meanwhile, grease and lightly flour a 9x5x3-inch loaf pan. Combine flour, baking powder, and salt. Set aside.

In a large mixing bowl beat butter with an electric mixer on medium to high speed about 30 seconds or till softened. Gradually add sugar, *2 tablespoons* at a time, beating on medium speed about 6 minutes or till very light and fluffy. Add orange peel and vanilla. Add eggs, one at a time, beating on low speed 1 minute after each addition and scraping bowl frequently. Gradually add flour mixture, beating on low speed just till combined. Stir in pecans and currants, raisins, and/or dried cherries. Pour batter into prepared pan.

Bake in a 325° oven for 55 to 65 minutes or till a wooden toothpick inserted in center comes out clean. Cool in pan on wire rack for 15 minutes. Remove from pan; cool completely on wire rack. Drizzle with Orange Icing. Makes 10 to 12 servings.

Orange Icing: In a small mixing bowl stir together ½ cup sifted *powdered sugar*, ¼ teaspoon *vanilla*, and 2 to 3 teaspoons *orange juice* till icing is of drizzling consistency.

Nutrition information per serving: 430 calories, 24 g total fat (12 g saturated fat), 134 mg cholesterol, 302 mg sodium, 50 g carbohydrate, 1 g fiber, 6 g protein. Daily Value: 20% vitamin A, 2% vitamin C, 5% calcium, 12% iron.

CREAM CHEESE-POPPY SEED POUND CAKE

Cream cheese and butter team up to ensure a moist texture and rich flavor in this melt-in-your-mouth cake.

1   cup butter (no substitutes)
1   8-ounce package cream cheese
6   eggs
3   cups all-purpose flour
1   teaspoon baking powder
¼   teaspoon salt
2¼ cups granulated sugar
¼   cup poppy seed
2   teaspoons vanilla
     Lemon Icing

Bring butter, cream cheese, and eggs to room temperature. Meanwhile, grease and lightly flour a 10-inch tube pan. Combine flour, baking powder, and salt. Set aside.

In a large mixing bowl beat butter and cream cheese with an electric mixer on medium to high speed about 30 seconds or till softened. Gradually add sugar, *2 tablespoons* at a time, beating on medium speed about 5 minutes or till very light and fluffy. Add poppy seed and vanilla. Add eggs, one at a time, beating on low to medium speed 1 minute after each addition and scraping bowl frequently. Gradually add flour mixture, beating on low speed just till combined. Pour batter into prepared pan.

Bake in a 325° oven about 1¼ hours or till a wooden toothpick inserted in center comes out clean. Cool in pan on wire rack 15 minutes. Remove from pan. Cool completely on wire rack. Drizzle Lemon Icing over cake. Makes 16 to 20 servings.

Lemon Icing: In a small mixing bowl stir together 1½ cups sifted *powdered sugar*, ½ teaspoon finely shredded *lemon peel*, and 1 to 2 tablespoons *lemon juice* to make icing of a drizzling consistency.

Nutrition information per serving: 415 calories, 19 g total fat (11 g saturated fat), 126 mg cholesterol, 239 mg sodium, 55 g carbohydrate, 1 g fiber, 6 g protein.
Daily Value: 20% vitamin A, 0% vitamin C, 6% calcium, 11% iron.

BERRY-GLAZED POUND CAKE

This deliciously easy dessert begins with a box of pound cake mix and your favorite berries. Choose raspberries, blueberries, or boysenberries.

1 16-ounce package pound cake mix
½ teaspoon finely shredded orange peel
⅔ cup orange juice
1½ cups fresh raspberries, blueberries, or boysenberries
¼ cup granulated sugar
¼ cup orange juice or triple sec
⅛ teaspoon ground ginger
    Sweetened Whipped Cream
        (see recipe, page 22) (optional)

Prepare and bake cake according to package directions except add orange peel and substitute the ⅔ cup orange juice for water. After removing cake from the oven, place cake in pan on a wire rack. Using a fork, prick the warm cake several times. *Do not* remove the cake from the pan.

In a medium saucepan combine berries, sugar, the ¼ cup orange juice or triple sec, and ginger. Cook and stir till thickened and bubbly. Cook and stir 2 minutes more. Strain berry mixture through a sieve to remove seeds and skin. Spoon sieved mixture over cake. Cool completely in pan on a wire rack. Serve with Sweetened Whipped Cream, if desired. Makes 12 servings.

Nutrition information per serving: 222 calories, 8 g total fat (2 g saturated fat), 0 mg cholesterol, 150 mg sodium, 36 g carbohydrate, 1 g fiber, 1 g protein.
Daily Value: 0% vitamin A, 22% vitamin C, 2% calcium, 3% iron.

PEANUT BUTTER POUND CAKE

For a winning combination, drizzle this peanutty pound cake with a duo of delectable frostings—peanut butter and chocolate!

- ¾ cup butter (no substitutes)
- 3 eggs
- 3 cups all-purpose flour
- 1½ teaspoons baking powder
- 1 teaspoon baking soda
- ¼ teaspoon salt
- ¾ cup peanut butter
- 1½ cups granulated sugar
- 1½ teaspoons vanilla
- 1½ cups plain lowfat yogurt
  Peanut Butter Glaze
  Cocoa Glaze

Bring butter and eggs to room temperature. Meanwhile, grease and lightly flour a 10-inch tube pan. Combine flour, baking powder, baking soda, and salt. Set aside.

In a large mixing bowl beat butter and peanut butter with an electric mixer on medium to high speed about 30 seconds or till softened. Gradually add sugar, *2 tablespoons* at a time, beating on medium speed about 6 minutes or till very light and fluffy. Add vanilla. Add eggs, one at a time, beating on low to medium speed 1 minute after each addition and scraping bowl frequently. Alternately add flour mixture and yogurt, beating on low speed just till combined. Pour batter into prepared pan.

Bake in a 325° oven about 65 minutes or till a wooden toothpick inserted in center comes out clean. Cool in pan on wire rack 15 minutes. Remove from pan. Cool completely on wire rack. Spoon Peanut Butter Glaze over top and down side of cake. Let stand 1 hour to set. Drizzle with Cocoa Glaze. Makes 16 to 20 servings.

Peanut Butter Glaze: In a small bowl beat ¼ cup *peanut butter* till fluffy. Gradually beat in 1 cup sifted *powdered sugar*, 3 tablespoons *milk*, and 1 teaspoon *vanilla*. Beat in an additional ½ cup sifted *powdered sugar* and enough milk to make icing a drizzling consistency.

Cocoa Glaze: In a small bowl stir ¾ cup sifted *powdered sugar*, 1 tablespoon *unsweetened cocoa powder*, 1 tablespoon *margarine or butter*, melted, and 1 tablespoon *water* till smooth. Stir in additional sifted powdered sugar or water to make icing a drizzling consistency.

Nutrition information per serving: 412 calories, 19 g total fat (7 g saturated fat), 64 mg cholesterol, 348 mg sodium, 55 g carbohydrate, 2 g fiber, 9 g protein.
Daily Value: 10% vitamin A, 0% vitamin C, 7% calcium, 10% iron.

ROSEMARY POUND CAKE

Look for orange flower water at pharmacies or in health food stores.

1　cup butter (no substitutes)
5　eggs
2　cups sifted cake flour
1　teaspoon baking powder
1　cup granulated sugar
¼　cup honey
1　tablespoon snipped fresh rosemary or
　　1 teaspoon dried rosemary, crushed
1½　teaspoons orange flower water or
　　¼ teaspoon orange extract
1¼　teaspoons finely shredded orange peel
1½　teaspoons orange juice
　　Orange Juice Glaze
　　Fresh rosemary sprigs (optional)

Bring butter and eggs to room temperature. Meanwhile, grease and lightly flour two 8x4x2-inch loaf pans. Combine flour and baking powder. Set aside.

In a large mixing bowl beat butter with an electric mixer on medium to high speed for 30 seconds or till softened. Gradually add sugar, *2 tablespoons* at a time, beating on medium speed about 6 minutes or till very light and fluffy. Beat in honey. Add eggs, one at a time, beating on low to medium speed 1 minute after each addition and scraping bowl frequently. (Batter may look slightly curdled.) Gradually add flour mixture, beating on low speed just till combined. Stir in rosemary, orange water or extract, orange peel, and orange juice. Pour batter into prepared pans.

Bake in a 325° oven about 45 minutes or till a wooden toothpick inserted in centers comes out clean. Cool in pans on wire racks for 10 minutes. Remove from pans. Cool completely on wire racks. Drizzle with Orange Juice Glaze. Top with rosemary sprigs, if desired. Makes 20 servings.

Orange Juice Glaze: In a small mixing bowl stir together ⅔ cup sifted *powdered sugar* and 2 teaspoons *orange juice* till smooth.

Nutrition information per serving: 205 calories, 10 g total fat (6 g saturated fat), 78 mg cholesterol, 127 mg sodium, 26 g carbohydrate, 0 g fiber, 3 g protein.
Daily Value: 10% vitamin A, 1% vitamin C, 2% calcium, 6% iron.

VANILLA-FUDGE MARBLE CAKE

Although not a true pound cake, this two-toned ring looks and tastes the part. Serve it with ice cream for a sure-to-please dessert.

2¾ cups sifted flour
1½ teaspoons baking powder
½ teaspoon baking soda
½ teaspoon salt
¾ cup margarine or butter
1½ cups granulated sugar
2 teaspoons vanilla
2 eggs
1¼ cups buttermilk or sour milk*
⅔ cup chocolate-flavored syrup
Semisweet Chocolate Icing

Grease and lightly flour a 10-inch fluted tube pan. Combine flour, baking powder, baking soda, and salt. Set aside.

In large mixing bowl beat margarine or butter on low to medium speed with an electric mixer about 30 seconds. Add sugar and vanilla; beat till fluffy. Add eggs, one at a time, beating on low to medium speed 1 minute after each addition and scraping bowl frequently. Add flour mixture and buttermilk or sour milk alternately to beaten mixture, beating at low speed after each addition just till combined. Reserve *2 cups* batter. Turn remaining batter into prepared pan.

In small mixing bowl combine chocolate-flavored syrup and reserved 2 cups batter. Beat at low speed till well combined. Pour chocolate batter over vanilla batter in pan. Do not mix.

Bake in a 350° oven about 50 minutes or till wooden toothpick inserted near center comes out clean. Cool 15 minutes on wire rack. Remove from pan; cool completely on wire rack. Drizzle cake with Semisweet Chocolate Icing. Makes 12 servings.

Semisweet Chocolate Icing: In small saucepan heat ½ cup *semisweet chocolate pieces*, 2 tablespoons *margarine or butter*, 1 tablespoon *light corn syrup*, and ¼ teaspoon *vanilla* over low heat, stirring till chocolate melts and mixture is smooth. Use immediately.

Note: For sour milk, place 4 teaspoons lemon juice or vinegar in a measuring cup. Add enough whole milk to equal 1¼ cups.

Nutrition information per serving: 412 calories, 17 g total fat (3 g saturated fat), 36 mg cholesterol, 391 mg sodium, 63 g carbohydrate, 1 g fiber, 5 g protein.
Daily Value: 18% vitamin A, 0% vitamin C, 7% calcium, 13% iron.

*Keep track of your daily
nutrition needs by using the
information we provide at
the end of each recipe.
We've analyzed the nutri-
tional content of each recipe
serving for you. When a
recipe gives an ingredient
substitution, we used the
first choice in the analysis.
If it makes a range of servings (such as 4 to 6), we
used the smallest number.
Ingredients listed as optional weren't included in the
calculations.*

METRIC COOKING HINTS

By making a few conversions, cooks in Australia, Canada, and the United Kingdom can use the recipes in Better Homes and Gardens® *Cakes* with confidence. The charts on this page provide a guide for converting measurements from the U.S. customary system, which is used throughout this book, to the imperial and metric systems. There also is a conversion table for oven temperatures to accommodate the differences in oven calibrations.

Volume and Weight: Americans traditionally use cup measures for liquid and solid ingredients. The chart (top right) shows the approximate imperial and metric equivalents. If you are accustomed to weighing solid ingredients, here are some helpful approximate equivalents.
- 1 cup butter, caster sugar, or rice = 8 ounces = about 250 grams
- 1 cup flour = 4 ounces = about 125 grams
- 1 cup icing sugar = 5 ounces = about 150 grams

Spoon measures are used for smaller amounts of ingredients. Although the size of the tablespoon varies slightly among countries, for practical purposes and for recipes in this book, a straight substitution is all that's necessary.

Measurements made using cups or spoons should always be level, unless stated otherwise.

Product Differences: Most of the ingredients called for in the recipes in this book are available in English-speaking countries. However, some are known by different names. Here are some common American ingredients and their possible counterparts:
- Sugar is granulated or caster sugar.
- Powdered sugar is icing sugar.
- All-purpose flour is plain household flour or white flour. When self-rising flour is used in place of all-purpose flour in a recipe that calls for leavening, omit the leavening agent (baking soda or baking powder) and salt.
- Light corn syrup is golden syrup.
- Cornstarch is cornflour.
- Baking soda is bicarbonate of soda.
- Vanilla is vanilla essence.

USEFUL EQUIVALENTS

⅛ teaspoon = 0.5 ml
¼ teaspoon = 1 ml
½ teaspoon = 2 ml
1 teaspoon = 5 ml
¼ cup = 2 fluid ounces = 50 ml
⅓ cup = 3 fluid ounces = 75 ml
½ cup = 4 fluid ounces = 125 ml
⅔ cup = 5 fluid ounces = 150 ml
¾ cup = 6 fluid ounces = 175 ml
1 cup = 8 fluid ounces = 250 ml
2 cups = 1 pint
2 pints = 1 litre
½ inch = 1 centimetre
1 inch = 2 centimetres

BAKING PAN SIZES

American	Metric
8x1½-inch round baking pan	20x4-centimetre sandwich or cake tin
9x1½-inch round baking pan	23x3.5-centimetre sandwich or cake tin
11x7x1½-inch baking pan	28x18x4-centimetre baking pan
13x9x2-inch baking pan	32.5x23x5-centimetre baking pan
2-quart rectangular baking dish	30x19x5-centimetre baking pan
15x10x2-inch baking pan	38x25.5x2.5-centimetre baking pan (Swiss roll tin)
9-inch pie plate	22x4- or 23x4-centimetre pie plate
7- or 8-inch springform pan	18- or 20-centimetre springform or loose-bottom cake tin
9x5x3-inch loaf pan	23x13x6-centimetre or 2-pound narrow loaf pan or paté tin
1½-quart casserole	1.5-litre casserole
2-quart casserole	2-litre casserole

OVEN TEMPERATURE EQUIVALENTS

Fahrenheit Setting	Celsius Setting*	Gas Setting
300°F	150°C	Gas Mark 2
325°F	160°C	Gas Mark 3
350°F	180°C	Gas Mark 4
375°F	190°C	Gas Mark 5
400°F	200°C	Gas Mark 6
425°F	220°C	Gas Mark 7
450°F	230°C	Gas Mark 8
Broil		Grill

Electric and gas ovens may be calibrated using Celsius. However, increase the Celsius setting 10 to 20 degrees when cooking above 160°C with an electric oven. For convection or forced-air ovens (gas or electric), lower the temperature setting 10°C when cooking at all heat levels.